MAI WAVES

*How to Build a
Successful Coaching Business
During the Coaching Tsunami*

DUSTIN VICE

Edited by Dr. Corey Lee Lewis

Copyright © 2014 by Dustin Vice
All rights reserved. This book or any portion thereof
may not be reproduced or used in any manner whatsoever
without the express written permission of the publisher
except for the use of brief quotations in a book review.
Printed in the United States of America

First Printing, 2014

ISBN-10: 1505867983
ISBN-13: 9781505867985

650 Productions
930 Lincoln Ave
Palo Alto, CA 94301
www.650Productions.com

Your Free Gifts

Included with this Book are Two **Powerful** Gifts to **Change** Your Life & Your Business

BONUS #1 Private One-on-One Strategy Session with Dustin Vice

CLAIM YOUR GIFT NOW

www.AllianceCoachingSystem.com/Session

BONUS #2 "Coaching Machine" Trance Meditation MP3 Download

Shift the Processes of Your Unconscious Mind Through this Hypnosis Recording to Dramatically Improve Your Skills, Confidence, and Success in Your Coaching Business

CLAIM YOUR GIFT NOW
www.MakingWavesTheBook.com/Downloads

Thank You!

Dedication

To Dr. Richard Bandler for creating a powerful technology that has transformed my experience and the world at large. Also for being one of the most hilarious and entertaining people I have ever met. Most of all for turning my world upside down and inside out. And as a result influencing me to change to be the best I can while always becoming better than I was the day before.

To John & Kathleen La Valle for NLP® Seminars International©, the Society of NLP®, and for their tremendous support over the years.

To Barbara Puffin, to whom I endearingly refer to as my *"Partner in Crime,"* without you none of this would have been possible.

To my late Grandmother, Helen Vice, Deborah Romary, Gary Woolman, Meadow Linden, Helen Lingard, & Dr. James Hardt. Thank you all for believing in me more than I did in myself at times and your contributions to making this dream a reality.

To Dr. Corey Lewis, James Dahlin, Armen Ra, and Owen Fitzpatrick for their magical expertise in breathing life into this work.

Much Love and Appreciation

CONTENTS

Foreword
Preface
The Purpose of this Book

Part 1: The Components

Your Job Description
2 Parts Client, 1 Part Coach, 1 Party System, 1 Big Universe
Building the Coaching Machine Inside
Mentors & Education

Part 2: How to Bring it All Together

Where to Begin
Pre-Game
The Complimentary Session aka The Sales Call
Align, Plan, Implement, & Measure
Practice Management

Part 3: Building Momentum

Speak
Merge with the Bigger Vision

Conclusion
Post Script from the Editor
Recommended Resources
About the Author

FOREWORD
Dr. Richard Bandler

I have long been of the opinion that NLP books need to sound less like NLP and more like people. What Dustin has done here is lay out a plan for those coaching others in life to do NLP rather than parrot terminology and rules. I started NLP with the idea that you could extract success from behaviors that worked separate from the theories of those doing it. Dustin has presented the complex as a simply well written new look at what we all really should know about the obvious. Which of course always has remained quite elusive.

Dr. Richard Bandler
Co-Creator of Neuro Linguistic Programing®
www.RichardBandler.com

FOREWORD
Owen Fitzpatrick

Since I first started working with people as a teenager in the early 1990's, the personal development field has exploded. The coaching industry itself is a gigantic market. When I began, the strategies that worked were word-of-mouth and perhaps putting your ad in newspapers or the telephone book then hoping people would come calling. Back then, there wasn't much competition. If you did a good job people would find out.

Nowadays, everything has radically changed. Coaches are everywhere and social media seems full of coach after coach screaming out their credentials and skills… offering you an opportunity to get your head in order, to get your life in order. There are so many options for people. How do you stand out?

Coaching is so popular because, when the coach is skilled, the process works. And it makes a big difference to people's lives, if you've trained with good people and you've worked hard at your craft. In buying this book, I'm assuming you highly value how effective you are. Because no book or strategy can help you, if you don't have the skills.

At the same time, what I really like about *Making Waves* is that it fundamentally is written to help you build a thriving practice. There are tons of books out there with suggestions on how to become a good coach. But it's also pointless becoming good if you don't have any clients.

Rather than simply motivating you to work hard, this book shares with you some fundamental steps that will help you to build your business successfully.

I first met Dustin a couple of years ago at a course I was assisting in Orlando. You get an instant impression of people. My instant impression of Dustin was that, as well as likable, he was a sharp guy. He understood how the business worked and he knew what was necessary for success. Since then, my impression of him hasn't changed. And this book, well, it's evidence.

Dustin has been trained by my mentor, the creative genius Dr. Richard Bandler as well as two terrific trainers: John and Kathleen LaValle. So he has been fortunate, like me, to have been trained by the best in the world. Spending time with him makes this quite obvious as well.

Over the years, I have achieved many of the career goals I set for myself. I have co-written a number of books with my mentor Dr Richard Bandler. I have trained people in over 25 countries. I live a life I love. But I made a lot of business mistakes along the way. Reading this book will certainly help you avoid some of the mistakes I made.

I started on my journey in the field of personal development eager and determined. What I lacked was an understanding of the coaching business. *Making Waves* is full of really useful information. Read it, digest it, practice what you've learned in it. It will certainly help you to build your business.

Then, well, it's about how good you are. And that, too, is up to you.

Owen Fitzpatrick
co-author of *Memories* with Dr Richard Bandler
www.OwenFitzpatrick.com

PREFACE

Obsession comes with the things you love. Some obsessions come and go while the truest ones stay with us over time. For as long as I can remember I wanted to understand how successful people were successful. I understood early on in my life that they must think and do things differently than the rest of us.

This driving obsession came about because I didn't want to end up like so many people around me. These people were struggling to live well financially, emotionally, and spiritually. As time has passed these people have gone on to struggle physically as well.

I wanted something better and I knew deep inside that if other people could be successful then there must be a way for me to do it too. This path of success is the labyrinth of life. You come in the same way you go out, and in this labyrinth there are no wrong ways or dead ends, only one path that leads to one center.

I have to thank those people who deeply inspired me to *not* become like them. I have had to go deep into the roots of myself to change who I used to be in order to become a smarter and a better person. This is a never ending work in progress. I also have to thank those who showed up as proof that the possibility to do better, live more freely, have more choices, and feel more joy, was alive and well.

Each of us, in some way or another is working towards letting go of what limits us and attempting to create the life we want. This book is here to help you do that very thing specifically for yourself, and so that you can teach others as a coach. Over the years of being a professional coach I have done things really well and screwed up royally only to come out the other side smarter. Sometimes with nothing else than to say "I'll never do that again." Now, based on both my mistakes and my successes, I get to teach you what to do and how to do it smarter, as well as what to avoid. I've designed this book to make your journey to becoming a successful coach easier and a lot more fun.

This book is made up of three parts:

"The Components"
"How to Bring it Together"
"Building Momentum"

Dustin Vice

THE PURPOSE OF THIS BOOK

"Until one is committed, there is hesitancy, the chance to draw back. Concerning all acts of initiative, there is one elementary truth, the ignorance of which kills countless ideas and splendid plans: that the moment one definitely commits oneself, then Providence moves too. All sorts of things occur to help one that would never otherwise have occurred. A whole stream of events issues from the decision, raising in one's favor all manner of unforeseen incidents and meetings and material assistance, which no man could have dreamed would have come his way.

Whatever you can do or dream you can, begin it. Boldness has genius, power and magic in it. Begin it now."

-Johann Wolfgang Von Goethe

    Humanity is in the process of taking a giant leap of evolution and coaches working in the personal development industry are positioned to be there to assist in the process and to become very prosperous as a result. The coaching industry, and this new era, are young and ripe for the picking. For those who are prepared and have the determination to succeed this is a rare moment of opportunity.

    Our job as coaches is to teach others how to develop within themselves strategies and beliefs that will get them to do what they want to do and to do it well. Giving our clients the freedom and the choices to do things better and smarter is one of the most valuable jobs in the world.

Human consciousness has shifted dramatically over the generations. For a long time we hunted and gathered and existed in small numbers. Then we started organizing the plant and animal kingdoms to our benefit and we thrived even more. We found new levels of freedom, safety, and security than ever before.

The curiosity of the mind drove us further to develop even greater technology to support our lives. We created machines and started mass producing through the innovations of industry which eventually developed into technology and information processing.

As a result of all this change we now carry computers around in our pockets as smart phones. We connect with each other in ways and on levels like never before, all across the globe, instantaneously. The question I ask you is, *what is next?*

The answer lies within you. It is a calling which is tugging at you. Inside, you know the truth of this expansion and evolution. You also know your role as an individual and a resource for others now and in the future.

The development of human consciousness is the emerging focus. The human mind is the next frontier of exploration. We tried to explore space mechanically through logic and rational thinking and were met with the limitations that govern the physical realm.

As we move into the frontiers of our minds and explore the role that they play in the cosmos and creation we move out of the lower body and into the higher aspects of existence. It is here that we really begin to reach beyond the day to day necessities of the physical being and begin to fulfill our purpose in more expanded ways.

In my opinion coaching isn't only getting someone to do something better. It is impacting the individual to improve themselves, and in turn the whole of humanity. One smarter person out there living a better, happier, and more fulfilling life will bring about endless amounts of good, now and in future generations.

As we improve life for one person we improve life for countless individuals. Each person is a part of a greater system as a family, a team, and a community. Each of us is related to the whole through our relationships with each other. You cannot impact one part of a system without impacting the whole. Although how you affect the entire system may remain hidden from your awareness, it is impossible not to.

Humanity as a whole has been in a very dark place for quite some time. The dawn of a new era has already come upon us and now the contrast of duality as good and evil is greater than ever. Now the contrasts of our world are more obvious to more people than ever before. And the well-being of the planet reflects that.

For generations the "powers that be" have been set on managing and controlling humanity and our consciousness because of their own scarcity mindset. Inevitably, as is true with all unsustainable constructs and limited belief systems, this mindset has already begun to destroy itself. The momentum of the change on the face of the planet is undeniable and has already reached a horizon point where it cannot be stopped nor reversed.

Imagine how much has changed in the last one hundred years. The population has increased by billions of people, electricity and technology are common in most of the civilized world, one can travel from one side of the planet to the other in a single day, we communicate and connect instantly worldwide through images and sound, and this list goes on and on. When you really consider the amount of change that has taken place during this time you understand how profound this momentum really is.

This momentum is not only growing over time it's also compounding. This means that the next century won't merely expand the same as the last century, rather it will multiply a thousand upon thousands of times the growth of before. The likes of which are incomprehensible to most of the minds on the planet today.

Imagine a world in which those that organize and manage it focus a great deal of resources into developing human consciousness and where the masses themselves are passionately pursuing their own development willfully and with delight, curiosity, eagerness, and anticipation.

It could be unfathomable to imagine a world like this because for much of recent memory, humanity has been associated with survival, suffering, sacrifice, scarcity, limitation, and fear. This new world is not the one you've seen in paranoid movies or read about in books. It is a world that is managed intelligently and cooperatively with consciousness, and the expansion of that consciousness is at the forefront of our pursuits as a collective. The world is transforming into one focused on well-being, creativity, abundance, growth, certainty, and clarity of intelligence.

The coaching industry is one of the many forces driving this transformational process of moving from where we are to where we are going. Your role as a coach is one of the major catalysts for how this will happen. The question becomes how many lives can you connect with and improve. And with all of the lives you improve how many systems do you impact? The transformation is already in full swing and there are large numbers of organizations and individuals that are in play bringing about this change.

The question at this point becomes, who will you be in all of this and are you willing to do what it takes to play your role? This commitment is not a haphazard one that you want to stumble into. It is important to be motivated for the right reasons. Your heart is calling you into action because this is what you were born to do.

You knew what was happening in this time and in this place. You knew with clarity and certainty that you were to be a guide, a teacher, a mentor, and were willing to go through all the necessary experiences to prepare you to assist others in their development, all the while improving yourself in the process.

When you know on all levels of your being that this is true for you and you are connected to this greater knowing, then this is the time to act. Not before, and certainly there is no time to delay. Excitement and enthusiasm are powerful emotions and clarity and certainty are even more important and more powerful. This is the state you want to be in when pursuing a place in the coaching world and working with others.

It is an awesome task to walk alongside others and to be a part of their development. It is also one of the most fulfilling experiences you can ever have. It's an opportunity to become more yourself, and to be a part of an emerging era taking humanity as a whole into the next level of its collective development.

PART 1: THE COMPONENTS

If you don't know what goes into a cake, how do you expect to be able to make one? In the first part of this book we are going to discuss the major parts of your coaching business, and how they work individually and together. This section will help you understand better what you are doing, and how to do it well so that you become a powerful source of influence. If this book were a recipe, this section would be the ingredient list.

The chapters in this section have been designed to expand how you think about what you are doing, or plan to do, as a coach. Try on each of the different components and play with them. It may be very different than how you thought of your practice in the past, or this may all be very new to you. As you become more experienced at handling the components described in this section, you will begin to have a bigger impact on your clients and more success in your business.

Just as a French chef plays in the kitchen with their exotic ingredients, play with these different components of your coaching practice, and learn quickly how to create a delicious experience for you and your clients.

YOUR JOB DESCRIPTION

"The person born with a talent they are meant to use will find their greatest happiness in using it."

-Johann Wolfgang Von Goethe

In my humble opinion there are two types of coaches. One knows a specific skill, trade or specialty very well. They know it on a level of mastery. They are familiar with the territory, the terrain, and the potential obstacles ahead.

This coach has been up and down this road a multitude of times and encountered a variety situations. They know precisely what you are wanting to do and how to do it. Even though times have changed they can very well guarantee that by working with them you will have all the know-how and support required to get done what you set out to do.

These coaches I refer to as mentors. **Mentor Coaching** is very important when you are entering a journey where there is something specific you want to accomplish.

Let's pretend for a moment you are wanting to take your product or service into new markets and are unsure how to do that. There are a number of ways you could do that. You could hire a marketing agency and they will sell you an advertising campaign and advertising space to go with it.

Or, you may hire a web guru and create a new website fully integrated with social media. He will explain in detail about the analytics of the market place, pay per click, and how to get your website to the top of search engines like google. He may discuss at length the value of building your email list and getting affiliates to broaden your appeal through landing pages.

Or, there's the option of hiring a new sales manager and sales team. Together you will create a rich incentive plan through commissions and bonus commissions for productivity and reaching new sales thresholds. Perhaps even bigger incentives like trips to luxurious vacation destinations for the salesperson and their family.

The only problem with these scenarios is that you are going to find yourself limited to the single idea that the person is selling, whether it is advertising, web marketing, or front line sales. In this type of scenario, when there are so many options to pursue, is precisely when hiring a mentor coach is the best place to start. The mentor coach knows marketing, sales, internet opportunities and most likely a barrage of other ways to get your company roaring at a rapid fire pace.

This person has most likely been an executive, may have run their own company, or has worked in a variety of the fields, which you will explore together. They will know from their diverse experience what approach or blend of approaches is best for you, and most importantly what sequence to do them in. They can show you what options are most effective and what order to do them in in order to create the most profit as quickly as possible.

Many companies and individuals waste valuable time, money, and other resources walking through a maze of opportunities to find the most efficient and effective way to get what they want. Some never even find it at all. Some get distracted in the process. Some get the result in spite of themselves. Often times they do what seems to work for others and what gets them the life and the business they are willing to settle for, all the while fortune and fulfillment lay just outside their understanding.

Think about the countless individuals out there with degrees and the massive debt to go with them working in restaurants and coffee shops. How many graduate to find themselves working in completely unrelated industries?

There is much value in going to school and trying a variety of careers. Often, when you talk to people who have done this, later in life, they say they wouldn't have changed anything. Many of them met the loves of their life, created a family, and still use much of what they learned in constructive ways in life. There is tremendous value in taking the journey. This isn't why people hire a coach. They hire a coach to get there more quickly and efficiently than they could wandering on their own through the unknown.

What I wish to demonstrate is that whether you are taking a product or service to market or getting an education, knowing the most efficient and profitable path to get there can be incredibly valuable and in many cases can be the difference between great fortune, massive debt, or even bankruptcy.

The second, and equally, if not more important type of coach in this context is the ***Personal Development Coach***. This coach knows intimately how the mind, the emotions, behavior, performance, communication and the spirit synergize together to create a powerful life experience.

This person can know little to nothing about your industry, work, or specialization, but by getting you performing better internally everything improves. These coaches work on the presupposition that you already possess within you all the resources to have, do, or be anything you wish, and as a result of getting your internal processes working efficiently your outer world will follow.

Think of yourself as having hardware and software. Your hardware being the brain, spinal cord, and autonomic nervous system, while your thoughts, strategies, processes, representational systems, and feelings are the software that runs inside the hardware. These software programs you have inside are what generate your emotions and operate your behavior.

Almost all of the programs running your life, work, and business are unconscious. Some refer to this as the subconscious. For our discussion that term is not accurate. Think about your mind as one whole thinking unit. What your attention goes to, and focuses on, is what you are, in that moment, conscious of and paying attention to.

The entire time that you are focusing on a particular, limited number of things the rest of your mind continues to be there out of your conscious focus. The part that you focus on in any moment, that you are conscious of, is your conscious mind.

The remaining part of your mind that you are not focused on is your unconscious. This demonstrates that there is nothing subconscious about it. It isn't under that conscious mind. It is merely out of your perception in any given moment. Confused? Read on.

Here is a great exercise to demonstrate this aspect of conscious awareness. I want you to think about your left big toe. Most likely before I asked you to do that you weren't conscious of your left big toe. Yet it was there in existence and you have no doubt about that.

Many associate unconscious activity with the breath, heart beat, and a variety of bodily functions that one doesn't typically consciously control. For the most part that's a good thing. This is because we are limited in the number of things we can consciously focus on, it is good that our unconscious takes care of these vital operations.

Although you can take control over your breath when you consciously choose to, the majority of the time your unconscious does this for you. Yogis, through training, practice, and meditation, have also learned how to consciously control their heartbeat and other bodily functions that most people are not able to.

The software running in your unconscious does take on the job of breathing, keeping your heart beating, and other vital bodily functions. It also runs most of your life from day to day. It runs underlying strategies of how you communicate, how you show up in your relationships, how much money you make, how you make love, tie your shoes, and open and close doors along with the majority of your behaviors.

These underlying programs determine both your success and what keeps you from succeeding. Somewhere in the past a program went in that said "this is how we do this" and "this is the result we get" and that unconsciously became the target regardless of how desirable or undesirable it is, or was to you. The good news is that your unconscious can be influenced to change, the question is *How?*

Here is an assignment: take a moment and relive your day thus far from waking up. Begin to think about how many activities you did with full conscious attention, meaning your full attention was focused upon them. Things like going to the bathroom, brushing your teeth, making or ordering coffee, drinking that coffee, driving or taking transportation to work or other destinations. Really consider how many of these things you were consciously aware of. When you think about your conscious activity you may be surprised by how little you are consciously involved in much of what you do.

I would bet that for the most part you did these things automatically through habituated neurological responses, also known as habits. It didn't take a lot of detailed thinking unless something out of the ordinary came into the process. This is a good thing when you think about efficiency. It's good that you don't have to precisely be involved in each individual step in your strategy. If you did it would take you an insurmountable amount of time to do what you accomplish in seconds automatically. Good habits are good and bad habits are, well, an opportunity to do things better, smarter, more effectively, and ultimately grow as a person.

Where these habits could become a challenge is when you wish to grow beyond what you already are and into something greater and better. A Personal Development Coach understands how these programs can be changed to benefit you and what programs need to go in their place in order to get more out of life, work, and business. More importantly Personal Development Coaches know how to get your unconscious to make these changes for you.

Whether I'm working with an executive, salesperson, or business owner, we always begin with the personal development coaching first and foremost. Mentoring and strategizing about business can be very powerful. It can also be thwarted by the unconscious programs we are running so seriously that our work is sabotaged. The likelihood of this goes up exponentially when the personal development work is left out of the equation.

This is why in our coaching system at Alliance Coaching, personal development and alignment of the unconscious and conscious are first and foremost before any strategy or implementation are pursued.

Taking conscious control of your unconscious mind is incredibly important to change. This is called alignment. The majority of the people on the planet simply do not understand how that process works or even where to begin to implement this change in themselves or in others. I would risk to say that most people don't even know that this is what is creating their experience.

Additionally even those that do know, aren't able to fully influence their unconscious for themselves. This is like a dentist doing his own dental work. Sure he knows intellectually how, but this probably isn't the best option for getting the work done. Especially if there is anesthesia or nitrous oxide involved. Better he get another dentist to do the work for him.

It can be very challenging to take on the role of patient and practitioner inside yourself. The same is true when working on your own unconscious. Like the yogis who learned to control internal processes in ways that we may believe to be impossible, they eventually learned how to do this only after being guided, taught, mentored, and transformed with the assistance of more experienced teachers.

Working on your own unconscious programing is possible and requires the ability to hold a third perspective of yourself leading the internal processes into change. Can it be done? Most certainly. Will you do it? Yes, you do already. Are you are aware of how you are doing it or not is the question. Is this do-it-yourself approach the most efficient way? For the majority of people it is not.

Coaching is not therapy, as mentioned earlier, for our discussion purposes there are two types of coaching:

1. One is **Mentor Coaching** which is guiding and teaching you to do something you wish to do that the coach is an

expert in. Thus, the coach can bring excellence out of you in this particular area of focus.

2. The second is *Personal Development Coaching* that will extract programs in the unconscious that limit you, your behavior, and what you get out of life, while installing powerful programs that will generate new choices in how you feel which directly affects new behavior that manifests a more fulfilling experience in every area of your life.

When the two are combined it is like two oxen, equally yoked, pulling in one direction. The fertile ground is plowed, healthy seeds are planted, and the rain, sun, and minerals of the earth nurture those seeds into a harvest of rich abundance.

As the unconscious mind and the conscious mind become aligned the outer results show up in all areas of one's life. This is the reason, I believe, that to be an effective professional coach you cannot leave the personal development aspect out of the equation. When coaches do this, they are limiting themselves, limiting the client, and making their job more difficult.

Our job is to make the client's life go with more ease, more pleasure, more enjoyment, and with exceptional harmony in their relationships more of the time. Why not do this for ourselves when working with them? We want to express our specialties and expertise, as well as, get the client out of their own way, and then get them into full force moving towards what they wish to create.

This creates a profound experience for both the coach and client. I'm always in search of the easiest, most efficient, and effective ways to do things. Over the years of working in this industry I've helped coaches build successful practices. What I've learned is that the only way to really get the client where they want to be quickly and efficiently is through first personal development coaching, getting them into alignment, and then mentoring them to create and implement the strategies for what they want to create.

Many times I've been asked what a coach's niche should be. To that I almost always reply that I do not find much value in declaring a niche, especially in the early stages of developing your coaching practice. A niche, not always but in many cases, places a limitation on who you believe you can serve. Say your niche is career coaching or health coaching. One day you are at a party and meet an executive or high level sales manager. Either of these individuals could benefit significantly by working with you, yet neither are looking for help to find a new career or to improve their health.

I believe that if you are really effective as a Personal Development Coach that you can effectively serve almost anyone on the planet. We all need to be smarter, think more creatively, communicate better, enjoy more harmonious relationships, and do things more efficiently and effectively with determination, certainty, and clarity. Most importantly we need to have more fun and enjoy more of life; our work and business will follow.

If there are things you do well and know alot about, this is a place for you to *market*, not a niche. It is a place to begin serving clients because there is an inherent rapport and you know with certainty that you can help them. As you build your practice and gain the respect of your clients they will refer you others to assist. Over time you will begin to notice a pattern of the types of clients you attract.

This is how I got into the business of coaching coaches. It wasn't because I had grandiose ideas of being an expert. It was because a coach was referred to me and I taught her how to sell, how to manage her practice, how to develop her business, and most importantly got her old ways of thinking and out of her own way. I installed new thought processes that turned into powerful emotions and activities which led her to wealth, success, and fulfillment.

As a result she sent me more coaches to work with. Before I knew it more than half of my clients were other coaches. One of my favorites sayings is "If you're looking for a sign, this is it!" I love that because the signs of what to do next are always around us. I was and am very successful with my clients--including the coaches I was coaching--and to me that was a sign to go further into developing the industry as a whole.

I'm still not setting out to create coaching coaches as my niche because there are many people that I'm called to help. Rather I focus on it as a place to do business. It also creates great pleasure for me to help others who are dedicating their lives to improving life on the planet. Knowing that I'm helping you to be more effective with your clients, creates within me a powerful feeling bigger than myself and that's what drives me to do this.

We are always going to ask our clients to go beyond what they believe to be true and how they think things have to be done. This requires that we do the same for ourselves. It is important to take our own advice, to take the good advice of others and to push the boundaries of our understanding. This requires us to continually upgrade the software inside us to be better, do better, and to live life in the knowing that we are always expanding, growing, and creating.

If you are a coach, and you are working alone without a coach, I strongly suggest that you make the investment to have your own coach on your team. So many times I ask coaches who come to me "Who is coaching you?" and they answer "no one." I generally respond to this by challenging them and saying "So, you don't believe in what you're selling then?"

Even if your life is going smoothly and your business is profitable it makes sense to make an investment in the very product and service you provide. It makes me wonder how much more productive and effective you would be in your life, and business, if you merely had someone there to challenge your norm and hold a mirror for you to see yourself.

There's a saying "An attorney who has himself as a client has a fool of a client." The dentist doesn't do his own dental work and the surgeon doesn't perform an operation on himself. The moment you think you've got this all figured out is the moment when the universe declares an opportunity to awaken contrast to give you the opportunity to reevaluate that thought. It can be a gentle reminder or a swift kick in the backside. Be careful what you think you know, flexibility is always key.

Perhaps you're asking yourself which of the two types of coaches you are. Perhaps not. What I'm asking you to do is to really focus on becoming as proficient as possible at being a Personal Development Coach. Do this by coming into an understanding of how the mind and emotions operate behavior to create results. Most importantly how to influence that process in yourself and others.

Once you are precise in being able to do that, anyone you come into contact with as a client will thrive because all of the resources they need to be successful are already within them. Then you can add to this the particular expertise you have and market from within this expertise, while remaining open and available to other relationships that present themselves.

There are two types of coaching that are performed in the industry today—Personal Development Coaching and Professional/Business Development Coaching—and again in my humble opinion it is in the merging and blending of the two that true coaching excellence exists. This excellence comes from assisting and teaching our clients to align their unconscious and conscious mind to create powerful change within them. Next, we assist in the creating and implementing of a plan based around what they want. All the while we optimize, improve, and catalyze the very best to emerge within our clients to perform these tasks to the best of their ability.

When you approach the world in this way you are now paying attention to the wholeness of the client's experience. All the most powerful healers, shamans, sages, and leaders from the past understood that the patient, client, customer, and the system that we are all a part of is already perfect, whole, and magnificent. They also know that the job of the practitioner is to align the truth of this well-being with the person that manifested them in their life while having the flexibility to influence their beliefs to allow it to happen.

    Now that you are able to understand the importance of your own internal mindset when approaching clients you can perform your work on an entirely new level. You can now think about how you can work from within and allow the specifics to manifest in the moment by moment experience. As you go through your experience allow the learnings and understandings as they have been presented here to ruminate, grow, and infiltrate what you already do well and make it better. Also allow them to go into those places where you can improve. As you surrender the intellect to the unconscious you have an opportunity to do for yourself what you ultimately want for your clients, create a better way of being and experience.

2 PARTS CLIENT, 1 PART COACH, 1 PART SYSTEM, 1 BIG UNIVERSE

"Every man is a divinity in disguise, a god playing the fool."

— Ralph Waldo Emerson

This chapter will teach you how to get your client to create an exceptional life experience and get results quickly. Much faster than traditional coaching and certainly faster than they would on their own. The reason I say that is because this has been my experience and the experience of my clients and coaches in the Alliance Coaching System over the years we've been following this process.

Most coaches coach in the moment and create a strategy and plan. The client then implements this plan with the help of their coach. This is a very good process but something is missing to make it even more powerful. We call this powerful component alignment.

Alignment is a multi-dimensional term that describes a multitude of elements all working together in harmony. This is when the conscious mind, the unconscious mind, the physical body, and all other aspects of one's being work in harmony to create through the quantum field.

No, I do not have a scientific explanation of how this works. There are a multitude of resources (many of which are in the recommended resources at the end of this book) with various explanations for how this process works but that's not my particular interest here. For the purposes of our discussion I will go into detail of how it works from the coach/client perspective and how this has worked successfully in my experiences and for those around me.

It is important to understand that within each of us is more than meets the eye. We are much more than this physical being that shows up in this world. Much, much more, in fact. If you are uncomfortable with that concept, it is likely you may want to stick to Mentor Coaching or stay away from influencing others in general. I say that because if you are going to work in the personal, business, and professional lives of others, it is important to understand the deeper function of the physical experience of life on the planet.

Each of us comes into this life with intentions, some more specific than others. This intention is our purpose for being here. It shifts and changes over our life as does the roles that we fulfill for ourself and others. Each of our challenges we attract as an opportunity, as growth, expansion, and creativity. When we learn big lessons we move on to the next stages of learning. It is an ongoing, never ending process.

Each of us has a soul, a spirit, or whatever you feel most comfortable calling it. The words we use to describe this true essence of us are irrelevant. What is important is that we recognize it as the eternal nature of each of us.

Our soul comes through into the physical body because it has a strong desire to come into this physical world and create in ways that simply are not possible in the higher, nonphysical dimensions. Whether you call that heaven, eternity, or dimension, again, is irrelevant. What is important is to understand that it is real and that the soul is real.

Most important in this learning is to understand we emerged into this physical realm and put on a veil to the other side in order to learn in ways that can only be done here. It is in confronting the unknown that we can truly understand and respect wisdom. It is in experiencing unworthiness that we can truly understand what true worthiness means. It is only in experiencing fear that we can discover the power of faith and creating certainty from within to shape, mold, and influence our reality. It is only in experiencing dark that we can truly appreciate light. It is here in the physical that we experience contrast unique to this environment and therefore can create greater understanding.

In this realm of physicality and duality we have an opportunity to grow the soul rapidly and deeply. The intentions we bring here are general in nature. We desire to learn how to create and manifest, to learn deeply on a soul level, and to do this with our family of souls that journey with us. The tough challenges, reoccurring lessons and themes, the repetitive dramas that keep showing up for you and your clients are a clear indicator of the work that is to be required to expand further on the deepest level for the soul to expand and grow.

When you experience life from this perspective you begin to understand that there is so much more to life than the problems and the solutions. You begin to understand that life's greatest challenges are gifts that contain the very growth, learning, and lessons to transform you on the soul level.

Whether these big challenges are being over-weight, financial trouble, expanding a business, getting your dream job, troubled children, sickness, or scarcity, they all possess within them powerful lessons. These lessons will transform your life and expand your soul into well-being. This is what we were after when we came into this plane of existence.

As a coach you have the opportunity to be a guide to your clients; walking alongside them in the awareness that they are going through this process as the larger plan of their life. When you work from this vantage point you are able to assist them to shift far beyond what they believe is possible and to assist in them creating seeming miracles in their life within a short period of time. Although these seem to be miracles, in fact, they have a clear and easy explanation: alignment.

Your client may be reaching out to you to help them with their profession, their business, or to get a better relationship. You will help them in whatever their perceived needs are and will work from this higher understanding and purpose. As a result their life over all will improve. The mind, and the Universe for that matter, are holographic in nature, therefore, you cannot affect one aspect without affecting the sum of the parts.

My clients, for the most part, all came to me because they wanted help with their businesses or professional lives. I marketed myself as a Personal and Business Development

Coach. More times than not, as a side-effect of the work we did together my clients would inevitably create a true love relationship. In some cases the relationship they were in was saved and improved dramatically. Others attracted their true love, either because they ended a toxic relationship, or because they were finally open to the relationship they truly desired.

I never intended to help save marriages or to help others create deep, loving, intimate relationships in their lives. It happened as a side effect of the work we did because I focused on assisting the client into alignment with their true nature and with the co-creative, loving, benevolent, and generous Universe or God. I coached them to get themselves into their well-being through enhancing their own soul connection and their relationship to the divine.

What is important to understand is that, as a coach, you are a catalyst. A coach shows up in their client's lives and you know the game well and how to improve performance. You have knowing of deep truths that they may not even be ready to understand or accept, yet you soothe them into their well-being, sometimes in spite of them. You bring them into themselves and get them out of their own way.

The way you do this is called a ***Coaching System***. There are as many systems as there are coaches out there coaching. Some work better than others and some have success with certain people and not others. What matters is this simple question: are you getting the job done at hand and on a consistent basis?

One of my greatest teachers, Dr. Richard Bandler, says you know a toaster works because it toasts the bread. It is a simple metaphor that makes sense. It is an easy test of your system. Is the client changing, and if so, are they changing to be smarter, enjoy life more, and make better decisions? Are these changes lasting over time and is the improvement from these changes expanding into all areas of their life? If yes, then your system works. If no, it's time to do something different. In fact, this is your indicator that you need to find what does work.

What I have found over the years is that the leading cause of someone not getting what they want from life is their thinking. Thinking is a tough challenge for many of us because we think a lot, continuously, in fact. Thinking is non-stop. Even when we are sleeping at night we think. I read somewhere that we think between fifty and sixty thousand thoughts a day. Regardless of whether or not that number is accurate, what I do know is that many of these thousands of thoughts are habituated and repetitive in nature. People are constantly changing, usually back into the same thing over and over again.

The thoughts, in the form of visualizations and auditory sounds, generate our feelings. The feelings are what drive all human behavior. Fundamental to any successful coaching system is that it optimizes how the client thinks, makes these changes quickly, deeply, and the changes are lasting in nature and affect the system to improve over all.

When you, as a coach, step out of time, and begin to serve consciousness and the abundance of resources that come from its experience you are able to suspend judgment. In suspending judgment you are able to serve from that broader perspective and really assist your clients where they are, and more importantly where they are going, one day at a time, into the future.

You, yourself, come into alignment with the higher purpose of your client and harmonize with their greater good. In truth there is no right or wrong, only the perfection of the expansion of the soul and the Universe. We all will make mistakes, screw things up royally, make a mess, and fall flat on our face. What matters is who you become as a result and how you show up in these moments of facing the inevitable.

When you serve in this alignment the real work gets done. More importantly you create harmony between all aspects of the self to allow life to manifest with more ease and less effort. It's like building a bridge over a canyon when you used to take switchbacks up and down the canyon walls to the bottom and back up again. You can enjoy the view and move more efficiently, by staying on top. And if you want to go down into that canyon and enjoy from that perspective you can too. The difference is you and your client now have both choices which equates to freedom.

This is the moment, in this powerful connected place, that it is time for the rubber to meet the road. Now, is the time to make decisions and take action. By doing the work to remove limiting beliefs and install new, more powerful ones you are now able to have the unconscious on your side. In connecting the client and soothing them into harmonizing with all aspects of their self, all orders of Providence begin to move in their favor. It is in this harmonic connection and their new level of certainty, clarity, determination, and joy that they are able to move into the life they desire.

If you haven't figured out what the two parts of the client are, I will explain them here:

One part is the client in the physical manifestation. It is important to understand that the body, all of its parts, especially the neurological system are all very, very important. This is where it all comes together into manifestation here on the planet. It is in the highest functioning of the body that one can have the most optimal experience on the planet.

The second part is the soul or spirit. This is the eternal part of each of us. It has a beginning and is on a multidimensional journey in and out of time/space, all for the purpose of being creative, learning, growing, and enjoying. There are as many varieties and combinations of ways to do that as there are souls in existence. We live in an infinite universe of possibilities and Earth happens to be the current beautiful place where we get to do this in physical form. Connecting to the soul journey and understanding that its purpose is to come into expanding as a consciousness, is the most important and vital understanding to have for yourself and everyone else.

Consciousness and its expansion is the purpose of our existence. How we each go about that is what we create through this unfolding. Certainly there are smarter, more efficient, and more enjoyable ways to do that, and really, as a coach, it is our job to assist others in discovering those ways. Become an expert in how to make yourself and others more intelligent and to have a lot more fun. It will make your job much easier and more enjoyable.

The third part is the Universe itself, also called God or the Divine. To say we are all connected is an understatement. It is much bigger than that. Not only are we connected, but rather, we are all made up of the same stuff. When one person hurts, all of the Universe hurts, and in turn when one part thrives, it all thrives. It is much like how your body works. When one part of your body feels something it sends a signal through the nervous system to communicate pain to the entire rest of the system, and all parts of the whole are affected.

Although many people have tuned out this greater communication, and are not aware how the unconscious mind works, it is still working, all the time. You don't have to be aware or understand how gravity works for it to work. When we get our body and mind in tune with our spirit we begin moving with the winds of the Universe. We begin to show up and respond to the impulses of these winds and navigate our life with greater purpose. Naturally we become ethical, humanitarian, and spontaneous. We become powerful in our gifts as individuals, knowing that we are unique while also being connected to the consciousness of the Universe. Knowing more than ever that we, along with everyone else, are moving together in growing the consciousness that is our Universe.

When you really allow this to become the core from which you operate as a coach you come to know that as you work with them, you are working with yourself. You'll understand this literally from the perspective of your own individual growth and also that you are transforming consciousness as a whole which inevitably includes you.

Now isn't that a job worth doing? You are a guide and for a moment of time you will pop in to walk along with others on their journey bringing them what they need. One reason you are so compelled to do this work is because it is what you do in the nonphysical. Your soul is also on a journey and has come to a point where it has accumulated enough experience to show up and support others.

The time has come for you to turn your focus diligently on this process, and make feeling good, being smarter, and enjoying life more your **top priorities**. Some believe this is selfish. They are right. It is a healthy form of selfishness. When you make feeling good your top priority you are connected in a way that will serve every aspect of your life. Life goes more smoothly and when tough stuff comes up you've got all that beautiful momentum there to support you through it. You can breathe deeply and know that the entire Universe has your back. Now, doesn't that feel good?

In all of this is the real purpose we are here: to expand our consciousness. This time on the planet is a rough one. This is a place of illusion, suffering, and where everything is temporary. We are torn from ourselves, from each other, and from our home. Things just seem to be on the precipice of disaster environmentally, politically, and internally. We have a handful of people controlling most of the physical resources on the planet and they seem to be determined to go to any extent to keep it that way in spite of their need for a healthy home to live in too.

It is indeed a matter of time between now and when we come to our senses and get our collective shit together. This handful of people, I call the controllers, will also come to this awareness even if that takes the planet purging us as a toxin from its surface. This is all temporary in nature and designed to give us the experience required for us to grow on the deepest parts of ourselves: our consciousness.

What each of us has is an opportunity. We have the opportunity to make a difference, first by changing ourselves, and second by teaching others how to change. If we could each make this our top priority, the world would change rapidly. There are so many at work already that we are building on a collective momentum which makes the task approachable and reasonable. If any of you reading this are in the unique position of working with someone in this group of controllers of the planet, I strongly urge you to do your very best to teach them to be smarter and to enjoy life more.

It is in this that they can come to the understanding that they have the power to take all of those resources and influence and shift how they use them to catapult our way of life as a species and as a planet into our next level of consciousness. It has been their means that has held it back and now is the time to flip the switch to transform how we live life. When you get billions of people moving in harmony with themselves, with the planet, and with the Universe, oh the miracles and healing that will take place. It is almost unfathomable because it is in such great contrast to how things are at this particular moment in time. The power of consciousness and the effect it has collectively on the quantum realm to manifest change is the only means through which our world can be saved from the guaranteed demise of our current trajectory.

Work from this perspective, knowing that you are a part of something that is much bigger than you. Know that the work you do is molding this new way of life into place. Will it manifest while you are still in this physical body? I hope so, though it doesn't matter. What does matter is that you are a part of it. We are the outcome of previous generations and it is time we come into awareness that the future outcome depends on us. Take this into all that you have, do, and be and let it work its magic now and in the future. Become the very best at what you do and live in the peace of knowing that you did the very best you could and that you are always improving from one day into the next.

This brings up an important question: Why do you want to be in this business? Really consider that question for a moment and answer it. I don't want the elevator speech. I want the preaching from the pulpit with passion version. In detail tell yourself why. What do you stand to gain? What do you stand to do? What are the consequences if you do not pursue your heart's desire to become an incredibly successful coach? Write the responses to these questions out in your journal.

As the leader of a successful team of coaches, I have the opportunity to ask these questions often to new coaches that join our team. Time and time again they respond with an elevator speech. What they don't know and I'm going to tell you here is that the most successful people on the planet know in finite detail on all levels why they do what they do and they can't stop from doing it. They also find great pleasure in what they do. They literally love doing it. Even after they make tens of millions of dollars they keep at it because they love what they do and know exactly why.

Each time I get these paragraphs from my coaches answering "why" I tell them, and I'd tell you the same, "Go back to the drawing board. Breathe life into it. Use your vivid imagination and give me the good stuff. Dig deep and go into great detail. Be honest, what do YOU stand to gain? Make it so real you're already living it."

Each of us operates from a system of internal filters of the world. These filters determine how information goes into our neurology and how it affects our decisions, behavior, judgments, values, and ultimately how we create our life. There are many kinds of filters.

As a coach the first step to connect to the certainty of your client's well-being is to suspend judgment. If you have a habit of thinking what is right or wrong and are inflexible, then this work isn't for you. There's nothing wrong with your client. What is "wrong" in relationship with what they need to change is their thinking. Your job is to be curious enough to find out how they think, and to help them change how they think and what they do and then optimize it. That begins with accepting them as they are and diving in deep with them as the soul they truly are and walking in their world.

As you become aware of the concepts we are discussing throughout this book it's important to begin to master your own mind through these understandings. Become aware of how you process information and in what contexts. Then, from this new awareness, you can begin to use these strategies to enhance your motivation around any behavior you decide needs work.

The reason why the most successful people on the planet are so successful is because they are being propelled by their "Why." They know in detail the good they stand to gain by accomplishing what they are set out to do and the pain and consequences they will avoid as a result as well. You will find this holds true for yourself. If in the context of your business you are very towards the opportunity of the pleasure succeeding will bring you, then by defining more of the potential pain you will find an entirely new level of motivation and determination.

Think of this as the carrot and the stick. When I wanted to lose weight, become stronger, and look healthier I thought about how good it would feel to look good, to buy new cloths, run into people that hadn't seen me in a long time and how surprised they would be and their comments, and listed all of the great benefits that would manifest as a result of my weight loss. I still didn't do the behaviors of eating properly and exercising, however.

It felt good to think about it, but for me it wasn't until I really thought about getting fatter and fatter, being alone, and dying a slow and painful death of obesity related diseases that I got my ass to the gym. In that moment I had a threshold experience and I couldn't take it any longer.

Before that point the potential pleasure was not enough to motivate me to actually make the changes necessary to get the result. I needed the pain, along with the good stuff, to stir inside me to create enough momentum to change the belief that I am someone who can't get to the gym into identifying as someone who eats well and works out regularly. With enough motivation, I changed the thinking, created powerful feelings of determination, and took action that transformed me for life.

I needed to think about the possible negative consequences of obesity: heart attack, stroke, social deprivation, rejection, loneliness, heartbreak, and ultimately dying young and regretful. It's funny, I never did so many things before because I was lazy and hopeless. But that's what worked for me in this context. Everyone could use more of the possibilities of good and bad to get them off their asses and start going for it.

It is in the identifying the good stuff and the possible consequences of not following through that propels us to become the person that behaves in a particular way to get what we want out of life. The good stuff draws us towards success and the potential pain pushes us away from failure. It is the mastery of each of these that will motivate you and your clients to achieve more and to do greater things.

The question I have for you again is why? Why are you in this business? What compels you to commit yourself? What pleasure do you stand to gain by doing it? What pain will you avoid by being successful?

When answering "Why," answer it fully from your heart. No one else other than you needs to know or understand what drives you. So be unashamed to answer with complete honesty. You are answering the question that will create within you a powerful source of determination and motivation to be successful. How important is that as a coach?

If you want to be rich and create significance, then write it down. If you want to be there to impact lives on such a deep level that their soul grows as a result, then write it down. Be unashamed by what truly motivates you. It is no one's business but your own and what is important is that you are compelled to do your work.

Answering why is where the rubber meets the road. This is when you will get real traction in achieving your goals. Many people make New Year's resolutions, write down goals, and even say affirmations and yet never achieve what they want. The reason for this is because they never took the time to figure out why they want these things in the first place.

The reason my clients and coaches achieve what they want is because we spend and a lot of time defining these important factors in-depth. And if you sit down with your journal and start to answer why and find yourself at a loss, then go look for a different job. You lack passion and understanding and have no business playing this most important role in a client's life. Sure you might have some success and you may even make a decent living. But, if you want to be one of the most successful coaches in the industry, your 'why' needs to be compelling and powerful. Without it you are an advice giver with a certificate doing unlicensed therapy.

What compels me to do the work I do is that it does indeed provide me with an exceptional level of freedom. I travel the world meeting interesting people, and am able to serve my clients as long as I have a phone line or an internet connection. Because of my level of effectiveness I'm also able to charge a significant fee, leaving me plenty of time to take care of my physical body, my spiritual body, my love and family life, and to have the adventures I've always dreamed.

The number one reason I'm in this work to serve you, the coaches, is because I know with my entire being that I'm here to lead and guide others on the journey to their well-being, their joy, their happiness, and most importantly to their love, worthiness, and connection to their inner being. The scale of the number of individuals that I can touch through this work multiplies by the thousands with each coach I assist in becoming truly effective. This is what drives me, my heart's desire, and my love for humanity.

The pain I avoid is in knowing that I didn't fail to show up to my heart's desire, my soul's purpose on the planet and squander this sacred gift. That my mind and body stay well and don't fall into the trap of sickness that comes with being disconnected from the spirit. I don't fear a fire, hell, and brimstone. What I am avoiding is getting to the other side in the non-physical and finding out I missed the point. I did not live my purpose. That I didn't live with enough laughter and love. That I didn't inspire anyone closer to their own well-being. That I didn't do what I intended to do. Worst of all that I wasted my life.

We live in a time when there is much of this going on for humanity. Where many are getting caught in the illusions of survival, duality, pain, suffering, scarcity, drowned in the intellectual ego, and the veil of the physical world. All of this is sacred and is teaching us on all levels too. The opportunity lies within each of us to come into an understanding that the illusion is only a mechanism for learning, expanding, and growing.

As a coach you have agreed to walk side by side with your clients as a way shower, a pathfinder. To teach them how their minds work and as a result how to focus their emotions in a way that impacts how they expand into their lives. As they change the manifestation of their lives they become more attuned to who they truly are. The key words are choice and freedom.

You may believe that you have experienced true wealth. And I'm sure you have. I promise you that it is but the tip of the iceberg. This is true for humanity as a whole. We have built amazing inventions, been to the moon and back, conquered towering mountains. In the end none of it will compare to the wonderful reality we will create when we, as a collective, begin to focus our minds in ways that bring about a world designed by hearts and minds that thrive in their most aligned state.

How lavish, how wonderful, how creative, and how much fun? Are you a way shower? Why?

BUILDING THE COACHING MACHINE

"The future belongs to those who learn more skills and combine them in creative ways."

— Robert Greene

My push for coaches is to influence as many people as possible. Quantity and quality are both very important. The reason I believe in numbers is because we learn better and more powerfully in groups. Also when you increase the number of people you help you improve the overall system. The system in this context is humanity. Systems also include, intimate partnerships, families, work environments, companies, cities, towns, states, countries, any central group that an individual is a part of.

What I have found over the years is that transforming an individual, one on one is profound, and it can very powerful for both the practitioner and the participant. When you combine that individual change with a group setting, the impact has a ripple effect, and is even greater. As a result you impact more systems more powerfully and more quickly.

You are building on top of a long legacy of transformation. Many have come before you and many are working now changing lives and improving systems all over the planet. There is an exciting collective hum of transformation rippling through all of humanity right now, making what you do more profoundly impactful and supported at whatever level you pursue.

We are in what I've heard called the "Coaching Tsunami." The coaching industry is flooded with "Coaches." Coaching is a generic term for anyone willing to give advice for pay. The industry is in its own wild wild west stage of development. There is little to no regulation of the profession and no real education or professional requirements are needed to work as a "coach."

Self-proclaimed coaches embark out into the world with a messiah complex to transform lives, meanwhile in some cases destroying the reputation of the industry. At the same time they are creating a lot of opportunity for those of us who are qualified, and who, more importantly, get lasting results for our clients.

Coaching schools and institutes are raking in millions of dollars annually in tuitions and spitting out "certified" coaches ready to take on the troubles of the masses. The white elephant in the room that few people are talking about is that these institutions, while many times providing good resources for their graduating coaches, don't actually teach their students how to build a small business, run a professional practice, sell eloquently and efficiently, and most important of all, how to truly influence the client to create permanent change in the deepest parts of them that drive human behavior.

I would speculate that more than half of coaching graduates never create a successful coaching business, let alone ever break an annual six figure income. I have yet to hear of a coaching graduate that has broken a million dollars of income in a year. Since there are few companies hiring coaches, the primary way to enter the industry is through a professional practice as a small business. This is why these missing resources are so very important.

For those of you who have read up to this point and are intrigued, resonate with the information in these last few chapters, and think this makes sense, read on. There's a good chance you are well on your way to qualifying to become a Professional Coach. This book is coming to you with divine timing to put you on the most efficient path to a six figure coaching business and maybe even a million dollar practice.

The question remains, *are you qualified?*

Here are some of the questions I ask coaches to confirm they are qualified to guide others into a better life. I suggest you take the time to answer them as well and to consider what the answer really means about your playing a pivotal role in someone else creating their life.

Are you able to demonstrate understanding?

In order to demonstrate understanding you have to first be able to understand. Most people think that understanding is listening. That is what we call a complex equivalent; like time is money. How does listening equate to understanding. Listening is part of the process, but it's only one part of the process of understanding. True understanding is cultivated beyond just what someone is saying and goes into what they are saying, how they are saying it, what they aren't saying, and ultimately the deeper structure of their neurological processing.

Understanding on a deep level is compassion. My definition of compassion is having the ability to disassociate from your perspective and associate with the other person's experience. Read that phrase carefully and contemplate what it really means; the other person's experience. A person's experience is much more than what they say or what you hear.

In some sense while we are gathering information it requires that we enter the client's reality, walk around in it and perceive the world from that vantage point. You want to really understand how they experience reality and how they process information. Understanding their world map and how they navigate their experience is the most valuable information. Listening carefully and <u>asking the right questions</u> will get you to the point of understanding your client on a deep level. Think of this as a friendly interrogation.

One of the greatest advantages of becoming a coach who understands others in ways they don't even understand themselves is the ability to demonstrate that understanding. This, in my opinion, is the most powerful ability in being able to influence others. Demonstrating that understanding requires that you have the ability to suspend judgment, blame, ridicule, and what you believe is right. This is not to say that at some point in the process you will not assist the client in doing things more intelligently and from a better feeling place. That will come later. What it does mean is that the key emotional state to have in order to merge into the reality of others is to suspend your own perspective in the moment to gather vital information to make the process of change powerfully effective.

When you demonstrate understanding to your clients and they really feel it is authentic, you will create a safe environment together, in which they can share the most vulnerable truths about themselves with you. This is when the real work begins. If a client says that it pisses her off to no end how her husband gets drunk on the weekend and sleeps away half the day, this is a good time to understand and demonstrate the understanding.

It is important that instead of jumping into fix-it mode, you instead move into understanding. Try their feeling on while staying resourceful. What must she be going through inside to get to this point of anger? How does it feel? What else might be going on beyond the anger? Then demonstrate it. Say back to her "That's a shitty situation, I've been there. My mom used to do that when I was a teenager after her divorce and it was really hard."

In that moment the client can relate to you and feel a deep sense of understanding. Now the two of you can walk down this road together toward a solution. It is one thing to empath the emotions and another to understand them.

Being empathic requires that you take on the energy and the emotions of the situation as your own. The difference, to me, between being empathic and demonstrating understanding is you go into the situation with a target of where you are going. I experience this a lot when coaching coaches and in the seminars I do. The subject will be going down this treacherous road of past trauma and those in the audience witnessing it will be empathically following along with them. The subject is in tears and so are those going along for the ride. This is an empathic response, and as the coach and guide in the situation, it is not resourceful to go for this ride.

It is important that we walk alongside, in a resourceful state, seeking to understand *how,* on a neurological level this is happening, and to demonstrate this understanding to the subject. This gives them the feeling that they aren't alone in their struggle and that what they are going through and how they are feeling has happened to us. When you do this you emotionally you build the bridge between where they are at the moment and the solution to help them to change.

Climbing down into a client's shit storm and wailing along with them will only further cause injury to them and it creates a high likelihood of injuring you. One of the highest rates of suicide is among mental health professionals and I believe the reason for this is because these professionals don't know the difference between observing, empathizing, and understanding. They unconsciously take things on without the tools required to stay grounded and to bring themselves and their clients out of the pitfalls of those they treat.

I'm sure you have experienced in person or in photos the image of a nearly perfect placid body of water. The surface is so still that it reflects perfectly the environment around it. There are mountains above and mountains beautifully reflected on the still water below.

The unconscious mind is much like this still body of water. Any sound, touch, or sight that comes into it affects it just as that stone that creates the ripple affects across the still surface of water. The neurological system is holographic in nature and any stimulation in one part creates these waves as pulses that travel to every other part of it.

We believe that we can watch the news, a traumatic experience in a movie, or have a fight and that it won't adversely affect us because we consciously decide that it isn't real or doesn't involve us personally. That's like assuming, however, that the skipping stone doesn't disturb the surface of the placid water. Every stimulus that enters through our senses has an effect on us and the people we interact with, period. Every thought and stimulus creates a ripple effect in the mind. Be mindful in your words, thoughts, deeds, touch, and what you do in front of others. Their minds are always open to influence whether they are consciously involved or not.

When you speak to someone, touch them, or demonstrate something in front of them, it has a direct effect on them. And when you do this with precision, from a place of really understanding them, it is like knowing exactly where to skip that stone so the ripple effect creates powerful and magnificent change.

The reason why it is so important to become masterful in understanding rather than empathizing, is it gives you the ability to feel into the client's experience and to build the resourceful state for yourself and them. So that they can move through the experience and to a new destination that will transform them all the while keeping you in a peak mental and emotional state where you can serve and improve yourself along with your clients.

Are you Successful?

For our discussion I would like to define success as a person who has demonstrated time and time again that they have proven strategies to overcome great challenges to create more choices and to have a high quality of life. This isn't to say that success means that you are perfect, never make mistakes, or lack the qualities of being human. Rather, it is what you accomplished in life that can amount to measurable success. How have you overcome your own shortcomings, and built a powerful momentum around mistakes? Is your life an example worth following? Can what you did to become successful be duplicated a thousand times over to create success for others?

If you think a certification will make you a powerful resource for others you are grossly mistaken. With a certification, from the proper institution, will come very valuable coaching assets. But at the end of the day it won't earn you hundreds of thousands of dollars on its merit alone. A coaching education is very important. Even more important, though, is from whom you get it, and what is included as specialized knowledge. Most important of all is who applies the resources gained in the certification and what have they done themselves with those same resources.

In my experience people who make the best coaches are transitioning professionals and successful business people. These also make the best educators. The reason I say this is because these individuals have the experience required to lead their clients to the best outcome in the most efficient way possible. They have been there, done that, and traveled down a similar path and successfully came out the other side. They know what it takes to get a job done and have worked with enough people over time to be flexible and adapt to influence their clients. Many of them have overcome very tough challenges internally and externally which gives them the ability to help on both the personal and professional or business levels. One cannot be separated from the other when creating a fulfilling life.

Just because you attended those seminars, got your certificates, and have given good advice in the past does not mean you should be charging a fee for your advice. The best mentors, which is what a coach ultimately is, are those who know the trade, the industry, and the most effective and efficient strategies to succeed from personal experience. All of this is needed in combination with the ability to influence the mind to transform as well. That's where the client's money is going to: your brain trust.

Are you influential? Are you a professional salesperson?

The first step in the process of getting clients into your business once you have gotten their attention is to sell them your service, also known as a professional relationship with you. And unlike when they buy that car or some other tangible item, they will not be driving home with their hands on the steering wheel after they buy from you.

We sell dreams for cash. Better stated we sell an intangible, the potential of an outcome, the possibility of their better self emerging. The client is paying for the hope that your relationship with them will lead them to an improved life, a better career, or a more successful business, a wonderful relationship, and better physical and mental well-being. In the moment it isn't tangible. They can't eat it, drink it, drive it, sleep in it or with it. In the beginning it is literally mere possibility.

The art of selling coaching services, then, can be one of the most challenging sales jobs out there. That's why I spend an entire a chapter of this book later to explain the selling process. In my opinion, however, it is the one of the easiest steps of working with a client. The real challenge comes after the sale. This is when the coach influences the client to change and become the person on the inside that is required in order to become the success they desire.

That, my dear friends, is a job of changing how they identify with their world. To change how they perceive reality and in many cases what they value and the priorities of those values. Talk about a sales job. People in many cases would rather die than change their identity. Wars which have ended millions of lives over the span of humanity have been fought over beliefs and identity. Our beliefs are the core of our identity and how we relate to our world. Changing them is the real sales job.

You think finding prospects or selling them your services is difficult? In order to become successful in the coaching industry you must influence clients to change. Change who they believe they are, what they are capable of, how they think, and what is possible. Most importantly to change the story they tell to themselves and others. This is when the real work begins. How influential you are will show by the results you get with your clients.

Are you a leader?

The most successful people in the world have mastered influencing themselves first. The side effect is they influence those around them. True leadership begins with the self. The most influential coaches lead from within and infect their clients with their own conviction, determination, motivation, and certainty.

Leaders know the art of how the mind operates, that through our thoughts we create our emotions. They are masters at focusing their minds to create powerful states within themselves to easily motivate the behaviors required to be successful.

Through this process leaders act as a powerful neutralizing element in most of the environments they walk into. They influence the emotional states of those around them and take a valuable lead in the dynamic of the people around them. Merely their presence affects other people to experience change. In order to be a powerful leader you must master the ability to build up the emotional states others need to be successful. Lead with certainty, conviction, determination, motivation, and an enjoyment for the process.

It is your own emotional state that first builds the bridge for others to walk over to arrive to their success, and then the words come out after to support the structure. When a master influencer speaks, ears listen, and when they give advice, hearts follow.

Leaders believe in the people they lead more than they do themselves. The most effective healers on the planet that span the ages of time all have this in common. They know with certainty of the well-being of those who seek their assistance. They hold the vision of what is possible and what the client's soul is bringing in to expand and grow. We don't coach to feel good about what we do. We do it because it is vital to our soul's path and to expand and grow ourselves as well.

Are you an entrepreneur at heart?

As an entrepreneur you learn quickly how to color outside the lines. How to bend the rules or overtly ignore them. In order to be successful it requires an air of non-compliance and to disturb protocol. The rules are designed to minimize your success, keep you in a ho-hum life that will result in just meeting your needs and dying in poverty. It's how the system was designed long before we got here. True wealth is being able to lose it all, and to earn it all back or even more, and that takes breaking the rules of the norm.

I'm not talking about laws. Follow the laws that govern the territory where you operate your business and your life. I'm talking about presupposed "Rules" projected on to us: ideas and limiting beliefs that are very commonly held by society about how to go about living life. Take an evaluation of the people following these rules and then decide whether or not they are worth living by.

What rules govern you and your relationships with people? Are you getting what you want out of life and your relationships by following these rules and beliefs?

Rules like…

You should have a plan B.
You have to go to college or university to be successful.
Stay at one company and work your way up.
Success takes hard work.
It takes money to make money.

These false premises are dangerous and are proven in many cases to be inaccurate and limiting belief systems. Successful entrepreneurs are designed to take risk, recognize opportunity, and are motivated primarily from within. They have a drive and determination that is unwavering. Their focus does not abide to doubt and worry. They carry a level of certainty that moves mountains and parts seas in their path and are unwavering in unfolding their hearts desire and soul's purpose on the planet.

Do you understand purpose?

These are but a few necessary qualifications for you to build a powerfully effective coaching business in my opinion. I'm sure that there will be the naysayers that will oppose some of my concepts throughout this book. This information isn't for them because they already know everything there is to know from their perspective and perhaps they are right. Being right isn't important to me. Sharing how I understand things to those that are here to influence others into living a good life is.

This book is for you. The person who was born into this world who has come to an understanding of the meaning of life and its true purpose. The purpose is to live in the experience, growing in the laughter, the love, the joy, and the pleasure of life through a profound sense of appreciation. And when we have big challenges or difficult times, knowing that in fact this is the juice of life that we came to drink. The purpose is to give others more choices, more freedom, and to maximize and optimize the opportunity we call life.

We came here to learn as souls in a way that you cannot learn in the non-physical. In the non-physical there simply is no concept of being unworthy, unloved, scarcity, fear, or discontent. It is not until we come into this physical plane and begin to explore these concepts through the veil of the physical body can we truly define what love really is. What abundance truly is. What it really means to know your worthiness. It is only in the shadow that we can define the light.

Each one of us is on this path of understanding and yes some of us are more in tune with it than others. Some of us are here to lead, guide, direct, and to teach others how to live more joyously, more creatively, and in a place where the bad stuff becomes good stuff to ignite us further into our learning and expanding. It is a practice not a destination.

When you reach the end of this roller coaster ride we call life and you make contact with the other side, free from your ego intellect, free from the limitations of this physical world, and you review the life that you lived, it won't be the cars, the cash, and the houses that you manifested that will be counted up and credited as the value of your life experience. It will be the lives that you touched and influenced along the way. It will be the small things that will stand out as the real accomplishments.

It's an awesome task to take on this role and it is not for the faint hearted. It has little to zero tolerance for fear and takes the utmost commitment, first to the self, then to the client's highest good. It is your path that has led you here and your number one, top priority, most important, VIP client is you.

MENTORS AND EDUCATION

"Tell me and I forget, teach me and I may remember, involve me and I learn."

— Benjamin Franklin

My education consisted of fine dining, selling and growing marijuana illegally long before it was cool, working as a financial advisor, owning a restaurant, and being a consultant/coach to many other businesses and business owners. I dropped out of high school and never went to college or university. One could say I took a less than traditional approach to life and my education. So what qualifies me to be a coach, let alone a coach's coach?

During the years of school I was bored. I didn't do well because I wasn't interested. Early in my schooling I was diagnosed with a learning disability. I even "failed" the third grade. The only thing that failed, however, was the education system and the teachers, not me.

The truth was that I started in one school learning how to read phonetically and moved to another school that was teaching through a more traditional approach. I wasn't learning disabled. I was confused. Understandably so, yet no one took that into account. The strange thing is that phonetics is such a jacked system you can't even spell phonetic phonetically. You can't sound out a lot of words in the English language come to find out. No one tells you these things as a kid. We teach stupid systems that don't work the majority of the time, yet they are taught like they came from the mouth of god, and when students don't get it, we blame the student.

Over the years I hid in my shame and boredom. The class I excelled in the most was Mrs. Steffan's. She was creative in her teaching style. She put me at a big special desk off to the side of the classroom. This made me feel significant. She gave me colorful markers to work with and big sheets of papers. She fed me jelly beans when I did my homework and made learning fun. She didn't fail me, she succeeded with me. I can't tell you exactly what she taught me, but I can tell you I remember her name, can remember her face clearly, and am grateful for the experience she created for me. She was smart to notice that I wasn't disabled, to honor my intelligence, and that I could be bribed into doing well.

These days, taking on substantial debt for a college education is common place. Even if you find yourself in financial ruin student debt haunts you all the way to the grave. For these reasons I'm thankful that my path never took me to University. My family was for the most part poor, at the best of times middle class, and lived mentally with the mindset of scarcity. There was not any money to support any educational endeavors nor would I have pursued them if there were. School equaled pain for me. In my mind that meant for me failure was inevitable. All this tied into my self-worth and what I believed was possible.

Though I didn't know it at the time, I was by no means stupid, rather I lacked confidence, skills, and carried around a strong sense of unworthiness. You may remember from the last chapter that feelings directly influence our behavior. It is our thoughts that create our feelings. If you feel incompetent, lack confidence, and feel like you're worthless, then you are going to behave that way and create a life that matches that.

These nasty un-resourceful feelings drove me to do what I believed I was qualified to do, sell drugs. Not nasty life destroying drugs, I sold weed. Marijuana can and does ruin lives. I do not wish to misrepresent that marijuana, like most substances, does cause problems, limits the people that consume them, limits relationships, and destroys lives. What I mean to say is that it, even in comparison to alcohol or even worse substances like cocaine or heroine, it's the more mild of the vices. Regardless, it was way beneath my potential, and even if I wasn't aware of it, the universe was.

Eventually that journey came to an end. I was pulled over with a freshly grown batch of some of the most sought after marijuana. It was Friday afternoon of Columbus Day weekend, which means I was going to sit in jail for five long days before I could see a judge the following Tuesday. This would be a life changing experience for me. Nothing particularly bad happened those days in jail. The change came from the *thinking* process it inspired. I was slammed into the reality of the consequences of my old way of thinking and the choices it had inspired. I made a decision, then and there, to never be in this situation again and to change my life for good. A voice in my head said to me *"There is more money and less risk in legitimate business."*

My life after my stint as a professional indoor gardener and entrepreneur was working in fine dining as a server. I did fairly well for myself pushing slabs of prime aged beef, over-priced Napa Valley wines, and bougie french cognacs. My co-workers had Master's degrees and Ph.D's and the student debt to go with them. It was secretly rewarding to be on the same level with them. I was surrounded by the elite and the power brokers. I got to know them well and their families. I was popular because I did a good job and was fun. We spent their celebrations, anniversaries, birthdays, retirements, and casual dinners together. I wanted to be them, not wait on them, but never believed that would be possible.

One day, one of my regulars asked me to lunch. I showed up thinking we were just hanging out. It wasn't uncommon to spend time with regular customers outside of work. I was often invited to parties, social events, or the lake home for the weekend. At the end of the lunch she offered me a job in her financial services company as a financial advisor with a salary and benefits. She saw in me things that I couldn't see in myself. She knew the potential that lived inside of me and wanted to foster that potential into realization.

She was right. Within a few months I was doing well. I paid for my annual salary and benefits in a single sale. It was her client, but I had crafted the proposal and sold it. When I asked her what my part from the commission would be, she said she would pay me a bonus of $1,500. To some that seems reasonable and looking back it was. In my mind a measly $1,500 compared to the $70k I had brought in was a ridiculously poor offer. Then I did something very stupid. I quit my job to be an *independent* financial advisor.

This was stupid for a variety of reasons. Number one it was her client I had sold, not my own. She had been at this business for as long as I had been alive. Second she took the risk of hiring and training me and I was greedy to not honor that. Finally it was incredibly cocky of me to think in my first year I could fly solo in an industry that is filled with cut-throat commission-only advisors on the hunt.

I struggled, that's an understatement, I went broke. The money was coming in so inconsistently and in low numbers that I was forced to sit across from my banker as she told me very clearly that if this continued that she would be forced to close my account. I did what most desperate people do when in unbearable circumstances, I prayed. I prayed with my everything. I did manifestation exercises, visualized, meditated, breathed, and kept getting back into alignment. It was hard. When you are faced with fear on this level whether it is financial ruin, disease, trauma, or war it is hard to feel good. When I did feel good I milked it for all it was worth.

Not long after the talk with my banker I found myself at a one-day seminar with a local business coach. One of my clients had invited me to join them. The lunch was sponsored by a financial advisor so he gave a presentation during the lunch. At first I thought to myself here we go again the usual dog and pony show I had seen a hundred times. Most of these presentations I refer to as "Death by Powerpoint."

He was different, however. He explained this intricate strategy, that when done correctly, would allow a wealthy business owner to legally exit his business with minimal tax consequences. My eyes and ears were wide open. This was fancy financial planning for the elite. Secret financial strategies that you can't even use unless you're rich. The outcome of the strategy was literally worth millions of dollars to the person who could benefit from it.

I didn't personally know anyone who qualified for such a powerful strategy at the time, but I knew that this guy was special and I wanted to know more. He was obviously not your curb level financial advisor trying to rollover your 401(k). He made rich people even richer and I liked the idea of that. After the day was over I told him that his presentation had fascinated me and asked if he would allow me to take him out to lunch, and much to my surprise he agreed.

At lunch I asked him questions about the strategy. I asked him about his business, how he built it, where did he focus, and what kind of clients he worked with. Towards the end of the lunch I said to him "I have several A+ prospects in my database but haven't yet pursued them because I was unsure of what I would do with them and what I would offer them. What if I invited them to meet with the two of us. You could work with them, I would assist, and it would give me the opportunity to learn from you. Would that be something that may interest you?"

He paused for a moment, which gave me the opportunity to fire off a fast yet lengthy internal dialogue of nasty self-deprecating things I won't even repeat here. I will tell you that it was the ugly and deep unworthiness and doubt and self criticism about why I even asked him to lunch to begin with. I was, in my mind in that very moment, an idiot.

Fortunately, my negative self-talk was wrong. Instead he said that he would entertain the idea, but first there were some things we would need to discuss before moving forward. He pulled out some paper and began dialoguing about what we would each be individually responsible for through the process of working with the clients. He detailed his expectations for me and outlined what he would do.

The next important thing we discussed was how we were going to split the inevitable revenue that would come in. I thought to myself oh, oh yeah that, the money. I had completely forgotten. My heart stopped, time stood still and everything froze around me. I felt just sitting in the room would be compensation enough. I was thinking "Oh okay if you are going to make me take some money I guess 3% is fair? Maybe 10% if you are really generous." At that point I didn't really care and I kind of wanted to die just at the mention of it. Here I was sitting in the presence of a financial god and feeling like I barely deserved to sit at the same table let alone make money from him.

Then he stunned me by saying, "So we agree then if you do all of this and I will do all of that, then I believe it would be fair to split everything... 50/50, as long as you agree to the responsibilities we outlined here, does that seem reasonable?"

I about shit my pants. How could this be happening? How could I be hearing these words. I didn't deserve this? I was a broken, broke, useless, a failure, a liar, a cheat, a criminal, and a mistake. I barely deserved to breathe the same air as him, take out his trash, or serve him dinner let alone split equally the benefit from a transaction that he ultimately would carry from open to close. I agreed any way and felt sucked into a whirlwind of confusion of whether this was even real or had I just imagined the whole thing. Maybe I was hallucinating and was having a flashback from my gardener days.

It, in fact, was real and a little over a month later I stood at the bank with a check for $57,000 in my hand. It was the miracle I had prayed for and along with it came skills that are even more valuable than any traditional education could ever buy. I paid off my debts and for the first time in a long time felt a sense of peace and worthiness I cannot even begin to explain. It was a beginning to a life that I had always wanted and deserved and in part I felt like it happened in spite of me.

The reason I tell you this story is because it is important to understand that you are both the mentor and the mentee and that your education is the most important thing you will invest in. It was more than just luck that put me on the journey that would intersect with one of the most impactful teachers of my life and that would help me to save myself from ruin on all levels.

One of the things that shocks me the most when I meet new coaches considering to work with me or my company is that they don't have a coach themselves. It may not be odd to you, but after having had the mentors that shaped me into who I am now, I couldn't possibly imagine doing this alone. Most coaches have experienced coaching, in most cases working with fellow students for practice. But, if you are wanting to do something and do it well, then work with someone that has done what you want to do and has been very successful doing it. It will make your life easier. They have been there and we have done that, been down the road you are traveling and can help you avoid the pitfalls, as well as, give you the short cuts and make it easier on you.

I started my coaching business by accident. I never intended on being a coach, let alone a coach of other coaches. I hired a coach years ago to help me with my personal life. She got me connected to the resources that I needed and helped me build a bridge to the new life that was calling me when the one I had was falling apart. It was an awesome experience, and even then the thought of being a coach never crossed my mind.

How it happened was that I was traveling the world with no plan at all really. I was free of any obligations or work. The work I was doing was on myself. Really, I was working on myself for the first time in my life. I had done a lot of work, but this was the deep work. In essence I think of this time as my metamorphosis period. I was working out, eating well, meditating, and changing those old nasty beliefs into beautiful resourceful ones--just as the caterpillar spins its cocoon and liquefies inside to be transformed into something completely different and new.

A friend of mine reached out to me to see how I was coming along on my journey. He also asked if I would talk to one of his friends who was suffering in his business. I agreed and talked to his friend. Inadvertently I sold him a consulting contract. We would create a strategic plan and implement that plan. He would pay me $5,000 down and a $25,000 bonus as a result of us meeting specific financial targets within a certain amount of time.

We started working together on the plan and eventually implemented it. Things did not go according to the plan which bewildered me. The plan was solid, a no brainer and simple to implement. What was going on that it wasn't working? I decided that I would interview the staff and find out what was happening behind the scenes.

What I discovered was that this guy was not doing what he needed to be doing as a leader of his organization. He was smoking pot, spending all day on his computer or phone, playing on Facebook and video games. He was quick to anger when his employees would make mistakes or screw something up. He was a bad example and leading with fear. As we like to say it was "No bueno."

After my evaluations were done I asked him if, at no additional cost to him, we could do some personal development work. He agreed. So I sat at my desk and began to map out how I had gotten to the point that I had in my life. How did I come from such an ugly place of feeling unlovable, unworthy, shameful, and broken to being successful and having the life of freedom that I did?

In our next weekly meeting I asked him a series of questions that I now use in our confidential client questionnaire. I used that information to find out what areas we needed to go into next. I had him stop smoking pot and start doing things every day that would improve his energy, and get him into an aligned state, so that he would feel good and get focused neurologically and emotionally.

Like magic he started turning things around. The strange thing that happened is very quickly after we implemented these changes half of his team left the business which he quickly replaced with better suited people. The energy of the business changed because his energy had changed and those old employees were no longer a match to this new energy left. Any business no matter what the business, its culture, and its success and failure are all a direct manifestation of its owner(s).

We succeeded in our plan and he and his business went on to thrive. I got my bonus. More importantly after I played back what I had been through it wasn't the consulting that I was most pleased with, rather it was the personal development work that had ignited my passion. I wanted more and was now ready to do it. I needed a focus and something to do with my life that had purpose and I knew this was it.

Next, I took the system I had created and asked two of my close friends to allow me to coach them as an experiment. They agreed and they too soon created amazing results from our working together. They did the work, they changed, and their life became better and they flourished. It was wonderful. They weren't perfect and never would be, but many challenges they had faced for a long time were gone and good things were happening in their life.

I was happy the day I quit selling weed. I was eager when I left my life in fine dining. I was elated when I left the financial services industry and bought my restaurant. I was deeply relieved the day I sold my restaurant and inspired profoundly when I decided to go out on my whirlwind international adventure. It all prepared me perfectly to do this work. The financial services industry taught me how to prospect and sell, as well as, manage a practice. Food service taught me how to serve, and the restaurant project taught me how to rebuild, turn around, improve, and to lead a team.

None of these things I did perfectly and in several cases I really screwed it up. What is important is that over time I got better and I continue to get better all the time. It made launching a successful coaching business profoundly easier.

After doing fairly well for myself I decided that I wanted to earn a million dollars coaching. So, I did what I did before: I got clear about my intention, prayed, meditated, visualized, breathed and got into an aligned state feeling good, calm, and relaxed.

A few days later I was at a grocery store in Bangkok. I heard an American woman's voice a few aisles away. I received a strong impulse to go and talk to her. At first I ignored it. During my time of metamorphosis I was a bit of a hermit. When I owned my restaurant and was in finance I was very socially and politically involved. After leaving that life I enjoyed being in a country where I couldn't even understand the casual conversations going on around me. It served me for the work I was doing. Because of this, it was at the time very out of the ordinary for me to reach out to another person, let alone a fellow westerner.

The impulse became so strong that I couldn't stop myself from talking to her. I introduced myself, asked where she was from, and had some small talk. She gave me her card and it said "Psychotherapist specializing in hypnotherapy." This peaked my interest and from our conversation we decided that we would meet get to know one another better.

When we did meet we spent hours together. We talked and laughed. Though we had a significant age difference we had so much in common. We loved helping people and were good at it. We were fascinated with how the mind worked and the spiritual aspects of it. By the end of the conversation she mentioned that her daughter had sent her a book and that she thought we ought to read it together.

The book was called "Get the Life You Want" by Dr. Richard Bandler, the co-creator of Neuro-Linguistic Programming® (NLP®). I had heard about NLP® years before but never pursued it because I didn't have a clear understanding of what it was. So I was both curious and interested in the book. Included with the book was a DVD of Dr. Bandler working on stage with several participants doing rapid trance inductions.

At first I was put off by him. Though he was in a three piece suit, he seemed unkempt and scary for some reason. He was mysterious and powerful and yet he made it look so very easy and simple. It is like when you watch Olympic gymnasts, they make it look so easy yet just the idea of touching our toes is impossible for most people. I learned years ago you don't have to like someone in order to learn from them. And I could tell he had some powerful things to teach me and that even just watching this short video had changed me.

Dr. Bandler created an entire field of study of the human mind. Rather than drill down deep into the root cause of people's problems he went on the hunt for successful people. He researched what they did to be successful and how they did it. He found people who were the best in their field and were getting successful results in changing people, and he modeled them.

He has dedicated much of his life to doing what these people did well, and doing it even better, more efficiently, more effectively, and has had profound impact on many. He has transformed lives, restored sanity, and helped the hopeless causes that everyone else gave up on. It is in his determination and tenacity that he has gone into territories of the mind others were ill equipped for and cared enough to walk in their worlds long enough to understand how their mind worked so he could influence it to change.

I read the book and did the exercises. I started incorporating what I learned into my coaching. Both my ability to coach improved dramatically as did the results I was getting with clients. Both the clients and I were changing even faster and the work was becoming easier.

One technique in his book that I remember clearly was how to fall out of love with someone. Before I disembarked on my international travels I had ended a five year romantic relationship and a relationship with my best friend of close to ten years. I used the technique to bring an end to both of the relationships, neurologically on an unconscious level. The flood gates opened and the real healing began. My wings were getting close to finished. Soon I would break out of the cocoon and take flight.

After I finished the book I decided to take my first NLP® practitioner course with Dr. Richard Bandler in London, England. At the time I'm not sure I can even really explain to you what I learned, but more of who I became as a result. Even though over the years I had done so much work, healed on so many levels, anxiety, unworthiness, and this sense of being broken followed me on some level. When I left London I had new techniques to use on myself and clients. What was even more powerful is how I felt. I felt free, unlimited, worthy, and that the world was mine for the taking more than ever before.

You may be thinking that this is when I started coaching coaches. This, like becoming a coach in the first place, came by accident. Coaching coaches actually started long before my NLP® training. Early on when I first started coaching, a colleague of mine referred a certified coach to me. I knew I could help this coach because she needed valuable information on how to design her practice and to sell clients.

When we first started together she was earning less than $30,000 a year. After expenses and taxes that isn't much. When you take into account the cost of becoming a certified coach she was basically losing money. Once we started working together, she quickly started experiencing more success, in both the results she was getting with clients and financially. Naturally she started referring people to me. Like I said before, like attracts like. Who did she refer to me? Other coaches. Rather than me pursuing this as a specialty or niche, the coaches were attracted to me because of the work I was doing.

Soon after I became a Licensed Trainer of NLP®, I brought my growing team of coaches to do a practitioner course with Dr. Bandler in Orlando, Florida. At a lunch with Kathleen LaValle asked if I would join the training team that supports Dr. Bandler's Licensed Practitioner Seminars. I agreed and have traveled to London and Orlando several times a year to support Dr. Bandler's work since then.

In case you are wondering, yes I do like him and I have a great deal of respect for him. We don't go skiing on the weekends together or play tennis, but what I like to say about him is that he is everything and nothing he appears to be at the same time and I'm not sure we will ever really know what that means. He is a guardian for information that is some of the most powerful technology on the planet and learning it has had a powerful impact on me and those I serve.

I also had the rare opportunity of being worked on by Dr. Bandler. I'm not sure what he was demonstrating at the time, or if he was demonstrating anything particular at all. It is difficult to remember because I was in a deeply altered state long before I found myself on the stage. He has that effect on people. I do know that what I remember the most about my experience is that I felt washed over by unconditional love and total acceptance. He installed in me a new sense of self-acceptance, self-love, and a compassion for myself. He also created for me a deep pleasure associated with teaching and speaking. Having overcome a speaking phobia myself, this was, and still is, very impactful.

What I can tell you is that I have coached coaches that were educated by the big coaching institutions. I believe that they received valuable information about how to work with clients as a coach. However, I can also tell you that teaching them NLP®, and my powerful system for managing and growing a practice and selling to clients, has had the single greatest impact on their success in my opinion.

Over the years I have attended hundreds of seminars, taught by many different experts, and been through a myriad of training programs. Personal Development, or more importantly consciousness expansion, in my opinion is the most important thing you, or anyone for that matter, can pursue. At the end of the day, and at the end of your life, your consciousness is the only thing you will take with you. In the meantime it is the center for all of your experiences and how you create them. Growing in this way is how you grow everything else, and if we aren't growing then we are dying. It is either progress or regress, there is no in between.

One of the ways I can demonstrate to you how big of an impact my coaching education has had on my practice is that when I started work as a coach, I only felt confident working with clients who were generally mentally well. The idea of working with clients with serious problems was an impossibility. The idea of working with someone with "real problems" like severe anxiety, depression, PTSD, phobias, alcoholism, addictions, or any other extreme cases didn't seem possible for me at first. Since I have been training in NLP®, however, I am willing and do work with these types of people.

The work is by no means always easy, but I'm willing to do it, I do it, and I get positive results and outcomes. These moments, when I have helped someone overcome a truly life-changing problem have been my most rewarding, and they are a testament to how powerful NLP® technology really is.

If you are deciding on what education will best serve you, be selfish and ask which one is going to have the biggest impact on the deepest part of who you are. What technology is capable of transforming you and the people you work with? How are you going to create the most success inside and outside? All the money in the world will not buy you out of suffering so you might as well dedicate all that you do to making life better and enjoying the ride more of the time. Ask your future self that is standing at the end of this life what was really important and pursue that in everything you have, do, and be.

When deciding on a coach for you and your coaching business or a mentor, work with someone you have a high respect for. Someone who shares your values or even has you questioning if your standards are high enough. You want to be inspired to be and do better. You want to work with someone who is doing what you want to do, and can teach you how to do it and who you need to become as a result.

The human mind is a fascinating thing. As soon as you think you've got it all figured out, it throws you a curve ball. This is why it is better to get it working for you rather than against you. Get clear, get relaxed, feel good, and all matters of reality will shift in the resources you require to do what your heart is calling you to do.

PART 2: HOW TO BRING IT ALL TOGETHER

Now that you have played with the different components of your coaching practice and have a deeper understanding of them, it is time to learn how to bring it all together. Hanging the open sign on your business without this next part is like knowing the combination to a vault without knowing what order to put the numbers in, how many times to turn the dial, or in what direction.

The following chapters are going to give you a better understanding of how to work your practice, get prospects, and sell them into your business. You will learn how to organize your practice and serve your clients so that they get powerful results consistently from working with you.

Behind that vault door is everything you desire. Most of all it will make your life easier and make earning a living on a consistent basis much more systematic. We call that cash flow, and it is kind of important to a business. The more you create organization and consistency, the better the results your clients will achieve, and they will grow your business for you.

WHERE TO BEGIN

"The secret to getting ahead is getting started."

— Mark Twain

Detailed within this chapter are the steps in the process through which you will get contacts, create prospects, convert prospects into clients and build your clientele from the inside out. This process is the foundation of growing your business. We have used this system with countless coaches, time and time again, to create six figure plus annual incomes.

The first thing to do is to determine what you want to earn. I suggest that you create an annual gross income target first. Be sure to include your costs for taxes, marketing, and support. You also want to pay off any costs you incurred for your education and certifications. For my coaches I like to start at a minimum $100,000 gross annual income. This gives them range and flexibility. Ultimately my coaches earn $250,000 and upwards a year. When you are one of the best in an industry or field these numbers seem more than reasonable.

The other reason for this income target is to enable you to live an abundant lifestyle, to have the freedom and choices you deserve, and to have the resources required to expand your ever growing business. If this income target intimidates you, make your starting goal approachable for you. For those of you who think these numbers are too small then follow that impulse as well. Be careful to not undervalue or overvalue your services. These are general goals for the variety of readers of this book.

When creating a target I recommend that you follow two guidelines. First the goal should be just outside of your comfort range, not so much that it feels impossible or ridiculous. It should feel like accomplishing this is going to push you out of your comfort zone and make you confront your beliefs around what is possible. Step just outside of the box. This place will become comfortable over time and will be challenged again when you go to raise your prices.

The second guideline is make your income target reasonable enough that it lives within the realm of possibility for you. The goal can, with some stretching, flexibility, and work be accomplished. There is this sweet spot between what we believe is possible and what is beyond that. This point pulls us into accomplishment. In many cases I have found that most coaches, especially budding ones, undervalue their services more often than overvalue. You are worthy of earning what you desire when you get results and love what you do.

Once you have your annual income goal, divide that number by eleven. There are twelve months in a year and I like to accommodate for a month of your year spent resting, playing, and for developing further into your trade. Also if you aim for a monthly goal based on eleven months and you meet it every month then what a nice surprise. I would rather have you over deliver than fall short and be disappointed.

Now you have a monthly sales goal. This is a workable number. If you are using the $100k gross annual income target then your monthly sales target is $9,091. This is the magic income number you're going to hit by the 30th of each month. This is reasonable and realistic for any coach that gets results for their clients and enjoys the work they do.

The next question is how many clients does it take in order for you to earn that? Now we get to start planning on what you will charge. I recommend charging by the coaching package, not by the hour. When you are charging higher numbers I've found that it is good to present and sell a complete package rather than give a number by the hour. Also you want to get results with your clients over time, build on that success, and gain referrals from them. Change work can be done instantly and the power of that change shows up over time. You want to build on that momentum over the period of time you are working together. What the client is really investing in is the process and the outcome, not our time. So make your compensation based on that concept.

Let's pretend that you have decided you will offer to work with your clients for six months, meeting once a week, with unlimited email support. And for that you are asking for $3,995. Which sounds more appealing to you, 6 months for $3,995 or $166 an hour? Both numbers are accurate. My experience has shown that people are much more likely to invest in the first option than the second because it inherently feels like a more reasonable offer.

Something also to keep in mind is whether you are going to get paid up front or are going to allow the clients to make payments. There are many opinions about what is the right thing to do. What I've done, and taught my coaches to do, is to give two price points. A higher amount for clients wishing to make payments with a significant discount for those paying for their coaching package up front.

What many coaches and prospective clients don't understand is that when a coach agrees to take payments the coach is financing their clients. If the client was buying a car from you, then you wouldn't finance them without a fee, if you would even finance them at all. A coach is not a financial institution here to make loans; therefore coaches should be compensated for financing and design their packages to steer their clients away from this option by charging a premium for financing.

Typically we charge an additional 20% for financing. We create an agreement and the coaching package is paid with 50% down, and the balance divided into monthly payments over a four month period. Not very attractive is it? There are a lot of financing options your clients have rather than going through you. And when you get results, enjoy the work you do, and assist your clients in creating profound results in their life the reasons to work with you are significant enough for them to find the resources to make it happen. You don't even have to take payments at all. Clients have credit cards, cash savings, corporate programs, retirement plans, home equity, their parents, as well as many other alternative resources. If they really understand why they want it, they'll make it happen. You as the financing option, in my opinion, really should be the last option, if you even make it an option at all.

The next step in this process is to calculate how many clients you will need to sell, based on your pricing and packages, in order to reach your monthly goal. Using the numbers from the example above $3,995 per client, per six months, comes out to 2.27 new clients per month to reach an annual gross income of $100K. We can round that up to 3 clients per month. This is more than achievable. If you don't believe so, perhaps you'll understand how after you finish this book.

Whether you get paid up front or take payments, a client is a client. When tracking your monthly sales goals a closed client counts towards your new client goal regardless of how they finance. What matters is you make your numbers. In the end you'll make your annual goal.

Exercise:

Fill in the blanks below to calculate what your goals are for creating a successful business.

Gross Annual Income Target: $_____

Divided by 11 months (Monthly Goal): $_____

Package Price and Timeline: $_____ for _____ Months

Monthly Goal ÷ Package Price = _____ New Clients per Month. This is your Target

The secret to getting prospective clients into your business is alignment, clear intent and planning, and then action. It is important you clearly identify who you want to work with, their characteristics, background, and what the relationship is going to be like between you two. Your client base is going to become your number one resource for getting new clients and like attracts like, meaning the clients you get into your business are going to refer you to clients like them. This is not a hard and fast rule, but there is a pattern of people hanging around with people that are like them both personally and professionally. This is why it is so important to decide before you embark on going out and getting new clients what kind of people you want to work with. It is also important for you to be able to articulately describe to others who you want to work with so they know what kind of people to send you.

Exercise:

Before you begin this exercise take four to twenty deep breaths. Do as many as are necessary to bring you into a calm, resourceful state, also known as an aligned state. Next connect your mind with your heart and allow your heart to take dominance in your energy. You may even want to place your fingers on the artery in your neck and feel your pulse connecting even more to the energy of the certainty of your heart beating and pumping blood through your body.

Once you are centered and feeling good take out your notebook and write at the top of the page "My Perfect Client." Begin writing about your perfect client and list their behaviors, personality, the fields they work in, and describe your interactions with them and what your relationship is going to be like. Be abundant, specific, and thorough with your list. It can be a working list for a while and will even change over the years as you build your professional practice and work with different clients. The more clients you serve, it will become clearer the type of people you want to work with and that are attracted to work with you.

You may even want to start this process by making an additional list of characteristics, behaviors, and interactions that you want to avoid. It's okay to do this from an aligned state because you also want to understand who you don't want to work with. We will call this list the "undesirables." What is most important, however, is that at some point in the process you describe the counter or opposite of these undesirables in your notebook alongside these things you do not want. Your final list will only be made up of items and descriptions stated in the positive.

For example, you may write down that you don't want to work with mean spirited people. A counter or opposite of this may be someone that is kind hearted or open to feeling good more of the time. This can be powerful processing for you on a personal level because it is good, in an aligned state, to declare what you are unwilling to work with and then to further define it in the positive. This changes the energy around your own personal beliefs. This multiplies the resources that you are creating through this process and points you towards the client you want to work with in the future.

After you feel like you have reached a sweet spot and that your list is complete for now, go through it once again and circle the "non-negotiables." These are the things you are unwilling to sacrifice under any conditions. Rewrite your list. Place the "non-negotiables" at the top of the list and again be sure that your final list is only made up of items <u>stated in the positive</u>.

Keep in mind that in reality your clients will **never** show up perfect. We use perfect as a target of what you are aiming for, like shooting for the moon and falling among the stars. Each person shows up as they are, doing the best they've learned up to the point of meeting you. They are human, perfect in their imperfections. Our job is to get them to do what they need to do even better, more intelligently, and with more enjoyment of their experience. This is why we have the "non-negotiables" and the general list. These are guide posts and will help you create a thriving practice involving people with whom you enjoy working.

Again this list can be reworked and added to over time. For now these are your guidelines. This process creates a powerful intention and focuses you, making your success even more powerful. You now have a clear target to move towards and a standard to gauge who you will serve.

Here are some examples from my personal list. Feel welcome to use them in yours.

Happy
Intelligent and demonstrates good common sense
Strong network of friends, family, and associates who they refer to me

They have financial resources to pay me my full price
They pay on time and upfront
They plan ahead
They understand and demonstrate that they deserve to be successful
They value my time
They value their time
They enjoy paying me
They provide repeat business
They are generally peaceful and kind
They want me to be successful and profitable
They demonstrate physical and mental well being
They express appreciation
They demonstrate integrity, loyalty, and honesty consistently
They have realistic expectations of what can be achieved and when
They want me to work only in my preferred schedule
They are decisive
They have clarity and focus
They are collaborative
They are sincere
Their value system and work ethic is aligned with mine
Open minded
Reliable
True to themselves
Praises me and those around them
Learner

Now that you know your financial targets, what it will take to achieve them, and who you will attract into your business, it is time to hang out your open sign and start building the professional coaching business of your dreams.

PRE-GAME

"Give me six hours to chop down a tree and I will spend the first four sharpening the axe."

— Abraham Lincoln

Now that you have a plan, know the goals required for you to build a successful thriving business, and are officially open for business, the next step is to get new clients. This will involve making contact and doing complimentary sessions with prospective clients.

The complimentary session is actually a sales call. You will need to demonstrate your ability to be charismatic, how influential you are, and that you are a powerful resource and catalyst for their change. This is a time for you to get to know your prospective client, and for them to get to know you. It is a time for you to come to understand how they think, if you both are a good fit for each other, and to persuade and influence them to make the investment to work with you. My coaches are required, in the beginning of building their practice to do two complimentary sessions per week. This averages out to about eight per month.

Many of the coaches I've met over time have good heart, want to help people and make a difference in their lives, and yet, they are scared of selling. Coaching is selling. As coaches we do more selling than sales people do. Most salespeople close a sale and then they are done with selling; a large amount of their work is in processing the sale itself and insuring fulfillment and customer service. This is not the case of a coach.

For a coach, the first sale is persuading the client to invest in the coaching relationship. This is sometimes the easiest part of the process. The real sales job comes out in each individual session. This is when you get to guide them and lead them into changing: changing who they believe they are and what they are capable of doing, their perspective of the world, how they think, and the things they do consciously and unconsciously. This continues each and every week, throughout the course of the relationship. Talk about a sales job. Wars are fought over beliefs and how people identify. If you think sales is scary this may be a good time to let go of that thought, let the fun begin, and enjoy manipulating and persuading others with integrity and their greater good at the heart of your intent. Ultimately that *IS* your job. And it is a sales job.

A resourceful way to think about this process is rather than selling, you are creating and developing a relationship that will last for years in some form or another and lead to other relationships that will build your business. This relationship is going to create a lasting impact for the rest of the client's life. The complimentary session is where you get to demonstrate how good you are at creating these relationships, at connecting, understanding, and how big your impact could be. When you do that the selling part of that conversation happens automatically as a positive side effect not a tortuous process. It really *IS* that easy once you understand how to do it eloquently and with integrity.

The first thing to understand is that this "sales job" is a two way street. Not only are they considering hiring you, you are also considering hiring them. You are going to commit a considerable amount of time, energy, and work to this person and it is *equally* important that you make the decision to do that. This also takes top priority over the short term financial benefit you may receive by going into this relationship. I, and other coaches, can tell you the pain and agony that comes with making money more important than following your intuition about hiring a client that you knew from the beginning was not a good fit. A "D-" client will cost you many times over what you will ever benefit in the short term financially. Build on our experience rather than reliving it.

This is the reason you want to be diligent when working on your perfect client list and sticking strongly to the non-negotiables. For example on my personal non-negotiables list is that I work only for financial compensation and I get paid upfront. I have had many offers for trade work and I've found that in this line of work a trade is too flimsy of a commitment when doing powerful personal change work. Though I may need the services of the person I'm working with I do not do trade work with them. I've found that this deteriorates the professionalism of the client-coach relationship, for me. Some coaches do trade and do so successfully. And having this policy has inhibited me from pursuing relationships with prospective clients that otherwise may have been a perfect fit. Alas I live with the short term consequences in order to create the practice that works for me.

The number one question I get from new coaches is "Where are these prospects?" To which I reply "They are everywhere, literally." This question, in itself, has a scarcity mindset around it. Asking where they are presupposes they might not be. They are here on planet Earth, obviously. Ask a better question. Asking questions is a huge part of your job. Knowing what questions to ask to get the answers you are actually seeking is the secret. Become a master at asking the right questions, at the right time, layered in such a way that there is only one path leading to what you desire.

There is no shortage of people that can use your help, have the resources to pay you, and meet your expectations of the type of people you want to work with. Once you make this your belief system your eyes and ears will open to them being everywhere around you. You'll wonder where they've been all these years. Believing is seeing (and hearing too). The question is how do I get them into my business and as quickly as possible? Where do I need to go? Who knows these people? These questions presuppose that they are here, somewhere, that it is possible, and focus on the results you desire.

The secret to getting these complimentary sessions is to make contact and in the beginning, lots of it with precision. Make contact with as many people as you can that could be your perfect clients or know them. In the beginning I highly recommend doing this in person. This means you will be required to leave your house and go out into the world, meet new people, and make new friends. Every environment where you are meeting people is an opportunity to make contact and get prospective clients to do complimentary sessions. The more contact you make, the more money you make. This is the law of the successful sales process. It is a numbers game. I don't care how good or how bad you think you are, if you meet enough people, you'll find your clients. The more you do this, the better you get and the easier it gets, so get going.

The reason my coaches are required to do eight complimentary sessions a month is two-fold. One, they get practice, a lot of practice. In a moment I'm going to go through the complimentary session process in detail and you'll discover that there is a lot to track and a lot going on all at once. To get really good at it and be precise takes practice. A lot of practice. Thousands and thousands of hours of practice. You will successfully sell clients into your practice long before you master it. Once mastered, you'll be unstoppable force of influence which will not only effect your sales game, it will also make you a phenomenal coach, partner, lover, parent, friend, and so on. Selling is influencing and influencing others is what we do for a living. We are the ultimate sales person.

The second reason is because eight complimentary sessions a month is the sweet spot and the magic number that it takes to meet or preferably exceed your monthly sales target. It is literally where the money is. I'm not suggesting that getting eight complimentary sessions is the easiest thing in the world to do, but it is achievable. It takes relentless determination, organization, and follow-up, and when you do it, you will earn the living you desire. This assumes, of course, that you get awesome results with your clients and enjoy your work. Track your contacts, follow through, and follow up. If you don't stay organized now, you won't be organized enough to manage a six or seven figure practice. If you can't manage a penny, you won't be able to manage a fortune.

You want to become obsessive compulsive about making contact with the *right* people. You'll notice the "disorder," as in obsessive compulsive disorder, is NOT in that sentence. That's because being obsessive compulsive can be a very good thing when it is in alignment with your heart's desire and kept in balance with life. It is a good thing to have ferocious determination and be powerfully focused on achieving. Having to lock the door twelve times before you go to bed is a disorder. Being obsessed about assisting others to become smarter and creating the life they want and deserve, all the while doing the same for yourself, is a very healthy obsession indeed.

You'll also notice that I put the word "right" before people. This is because you want to focus your time and efforts into getting in front of your perfect clients and not wasting time. Remember like attracts like and people hang out with people that are like them. I was told some time ago that people hang out with others that earn 10% more or less than them. Where does your perfect client hang out? When you answer that, go there, and you'll not just find one perfect client, you'll find many.

I have my coaches grade their existing and prospective clients using the A, B, C, D grading method from most schools. We eliminate all the C's and D's. Then we sort the B's into two categories. The first category of B's are the ones who can, through coaching, be upgraded to A's in a short to medium time frame. The second category of B's are those who will remain B's, and over time they are eliminated as well. It may seem harsh, but when your goal is to build a massively successful practice you've got to spend your time wisely and focus on not working with the people you like and only with people you love working with. Go for the A's or go home.

This idea is going to save you thousands of hours of difficulty and headache. Build on this rather than dredging through it. The purpose of this book is to get you to build your business better and more efficiently, from what I've learned over the years of doing this. I worked with C's and D's and it bit me in the ass.

A great metaphor for this process of making contact is making new friends. There can be so much pressure associated with the selling process it is a good idea to lighten up about it and attach a good feeling that compels you to do it. When you go into a group of new people, go in with the attitude of making new friends and that the complimentary session is similar to asking these new friends to meet for coffee or lunch. I don't suggest that you actually meet for coffee or lunch, though you can do that. These periphery activities can often be a distraction to the selling process for both you and your prospect. If you are going to meet for coffee or lunch perhaps use that time to build on your relationship and as result set up a time for a complimentary session as the next step in the process.

There is no right or wrong way for you to build a new relationship with a prospective client. There is the most efficient and effective way that works for you. The process I'm outlining throughout this book is what has worked well for me and the coaches I work with to be successful. I avoid casual public places for a meeting because I want as close to 100% of their attention as I can get and I want to give them as close to

100% of my attention. I have also found you simply cannot get the intimacy and vulnerability that you need in these types of settings.

A good metaphor for the selling process is a chain. The links in the chain are a series of agreements made consciously and unconsciously by your prospect that lead to the end of that chain which is them buying from you. Your job is to guide them through these links one by one as agreements.

When making contact it is critical that you lead the process. When you first make contact, be sure to collect *their* contact information. For years I didn't have a website or a business card. I earned six figures a year with a single page PDF, a good reputation for getting results, and being enjoyable to work with. Get business cards and pass them out as much as you want, but don't count on them earning you a hundred thousand dollars.

When someone would ask for my card I would simply say "Oh, I don't carry cards though I'm happy to take yours." Or I would say "Well I have a rule about that…" to which they would ask "Oh really what's that?" And in a playful tone I would reply, "I'll only give you one in exchange for yours." Many times people would say they didn't have one. In this scenario I would say "That's ok." And I would hand them my phone with it already open to the add contact screen ready for them to fill in their valuable information. Then I would send them my contact information via text or email. Your job is to get the contacts information, track it, follow up on it, and pursue them, not the other way around. You're a professional and your job is to demonstrate that from beginning to end.

You want to take control of the contact because it insures that you won't lose this opportunity to build a relationship. People usually don't purposely forget to contact you, they just get caught up in their day to day lives and the further they get into the future the more they forget to follow up with you. That's why, as the sales person and coach, you should be the one to do that job. It also demonstrates from the beginning that you are going to be a resource for accountability in the relationship and you are going to model what you expect from them. Getting your prospect's contact information and following up with them is worth handing out a thousand business cards and is much more likely to earn you a hundred thousand dollars.

One way to generate interest in what you do is to make casual conversation. People often love to talk about themselves and when provoked typically take the stage beautifully. What is the secret behind getting them to do so? Ask questions. We are going to talk a lot about questions throughout this process. Learning how to ask the right questions and in the proper order, is one of the most powerful skills a human can have. Focus your questions on where you want the conversation to go, on the target. Inevitably you'll find a hot topic that aligns with what you can help them with, but you will need to lead them to give it to you. Don't expect them to give it to you on a silver platter. Be the panther in the bush and be ready for the moment to pounce and the opportunity will present itself.

I have found that especially in the US people almost always, within the first few moments of conversation, ask "What do you do?" as an introductory question. This is a very common generic conversational question. It quickly defines your social caste and ranking. Regardless it can be a pivot point for the conversation. When leading a conversation like this with someone answer briefly, precisely, and then quickly turn the attention back to them as the subject at hand. How do you do that? Ask a question about them after you give them your brief precise response.

You want to dig up more from them so that you can leverage the conversation towards the complimentary session. Stay focused and on target toward the next link in the chain. You also want to create a certain level of intrigue. My answer to this common question is "I'm a personal and business development coach." If they ask what that means I give them my thirty second or less run down in simple understandable language and follow with a question that redirects them back to talking about themselves.

My response is something along the lines of: "I work with individuals and companies to create change to improve their lives or the system of the company and make things better." This is general and it leaves a big giant hole for me to fill in later. The reason I don't suggest going into great detail is because at this point of the conversation you don't really know what is important for them to hear or how they need to hear about what you do or how you do it. Save that talk for the complimentary session when you understand them better and the actual sale is on the line. For now, entice them into learning more and build the relationship with them from there.

Be careful of the times when this new contact is a little too good at asking questions. Sometimes they will take control and in our excitement to share about what we do, and their questions being so good at pulling it out of us, we get lost in our own repertoire. Nothing can be more damaging in building this kind of relationship than getting off track and sucked into our own neurosis. If required simply say "I would be happy to tell you all about it during a complimentary session if that interests you?" Keep your eye on the prize, the complimentary session, and when the opportunity presents itself seize it.

After you've established a friendly connection with them and things are flowing between you two, you may want to ask about what kind of challenges they are facing. Whether they are personal or professional, you'll most likely know what area to dig into by the content of the conversation you've had up to this point. People often give verbal and non-verbal cues about what is bothering them. Overtime they will begin to jump out at you like an ambulance with its lights and sirens on in traffic.

Once they've identified the big boulders blocking them, you want to first demonstrate that you understand and can relate to their challenges. Use a short and precise example from your own life. You want them to feel that you've been there and maybe even done that, that we all have, that they aren't alone, and relate to how frustrating, or difficult it is, or whatever emotion is appropriate for you to share with them. Demonstrate true understanding that is real and from a place of integrity. If you've never had a C-section don't say that you have. That's called lying. You have been afraid before about your physical body, been scared out of your mind, or something similar. Use these experiences to relate and be real, be authentic, and reflect what they are really talking about.

Once you've taken the time to understand their challenge and demonstrated that you understand, now is a good time to use the magic words to activate the next link in the chain. "I think I may be able to help you with that. I've got a couple ideas that I'd like to share with you, though, now isn't really a good time. It may be good for us to meet up for a complimentary session, if you are interested?" Then <u>close your mouth</u>, raise your eyebrows slightly, and *wait* for their response.

So many sales people don't understand this critical part of the process. I call this powerful technique "Shutting Up." How many times has this happened to you? You're going to buy something and you're ready to close the deal and the sales person keeps going on and on with *their* process. Have you ever gotten to the point where you actually didn't buy because of this? Sadly it does happen. Knowing when to talk and when to be quiet is the part of process I call precision. Precision is power. Knowing when to talk, when to listen, and when to provoke a response is your job in both selling and coaching.

You don't want to present an air of superiority or certainty that you will help them because that kind of language in itself is too rigid and can bring pressure into the interaction. Saying you will fix them infers they are broken and they have to do something whereas believing you *may* be able to give them some solution to what they are going through sounds more like an opportunity with potential. Remember to walk softly just like the panther so as not to disturb the environment and scare away your prospective client.

The next link in the chain is getting them to agree to a time and place. Since I've worked internationally through referral for many years most of my complimentary sessions took place over phone or Skype. I suggest doing an audio only call instead of video conferencing. Video is a distraction and isn't really necessary for you to have a successful call. In the beginning of your practice I recommend live, in person sessions. Doing this kind of work over the phone takes a lot of practice. Not that it can't be done, but I want to make things as easy on you as possible.

I strongly suggest, before you meet with your prospective client, you have them fill out a very short questionnaire with a handful of yes or no questions. Short, being the key word. Having them fill out a 19 page questionnaire is only going to hinder getting them to this vital first meeting. This questionnaire is to be returned to you forty-eight hours before your scheduled meeting to give you time to review it, and this demonstrates that you will expect a certain level of self-discipline and accountability from them. Here are the questions we use:

I am meeting my finanical objectives   Y/N
I am satisfied with my current occupation/career/business   Y/N
I am ready to break through to the next level (business/career) Y/N
I am satisfied with my romantic relationship Y/N
I am satisfied with relationships in general   Y/N
My relationships are harmonious and agreeable overall   Y/N
I am satisfied with my health   Y/N

This questionnaire will take them just a few minutes to answer, and it will give you the necessary talking points to generate a conversation with your prospective client. Be very careful not to make assumptions from the responses to these questions. Yes and No questions are surface questions. They are a starting point for asking other questions. Do you have enough information to draw conclusions about this prospect from this short questionnaire? No, you do not. What you do have is a launching pad for a conversation to go deeper into the information presented and this questionnaire, simply serves to break the ice and start that process.

For example, someone may answer "No" to the question "I am meeting my financial objectives." One may read that and think "Oh great, there's no way they are going to be able to afford my fee. There goes an hour or more of my life I'll never get back." But, this may not be true.

In the complimentary session you want to say to the prospect "I noticed that you said that you weren't meeting your financial obligations. What does it mean to you to be meeting your financial obligations?" This statement and question probes immediately into the bigger question beneath it, without asking the uncomfortable question, can you afford my fee?

In a real life example, I once asked this same question to a prospective client during a complimentary session and she said "Well I planned to take my kids to Disneyland this year. And as of where I am now, that's not going to happen." That client did hire me and as a result she and her family did go to Disneyland. I don't know about you, but I didn't think of a family vacation as being a financial "obligation." She did and if I wouldn't have asked and just assumed it meant she couldn't afford me, then I might have missed the opportunity of working with her. She paid for coaching through a company benefit and as a result hit her quarterly numbers and got a bonus that took her and her family to the magic kingdom. So much for assuming. As the popular saying goes, "Never ASSUME, because when you ASSUME, you make an ASS of U and ME."

Here's another real example about when an assumption didn't serve me well. I was referred to an existing coach. We arranged the meeting at her home. When I pulled up I thought to myself how was she ever going to afford me. An old Kia sat in the driveway and the house was modest and under appointed. Early on in the conversation she mentioned she had received an inheritance from her father who passed away not long before our meeting. That was how she was able to afford me. She got organized and focused and has since earned over ten times what she paid me to coach her.

It is important before you meet for the complimentary session that you do as much research on your prospective client as possible before your meeting. Check their Facebook. If they were referred to you be sure to interview the referral source and ask good questions about them. If you notice you have mutual friends check in with them too. Ask questions like how long have they known this person? What do they like about them? What kind of challenges do they have? How do they think you could help them? <u>Get as much information as is available.</u>

If you are prospecting a company find out as much as you can about that company. Read their website thoroughly. Find out if there is any public information available. Find out who the key people are and research them in detail. Find reviews from the customers and clients of the company. Do your due diligence and your homework.

The next step after you have made contact, and gotten the agreement to do the sales call is to gather information, as much relevant information as you possibly can about this new relationship. This happens before the meeting and during it. Don't be shy, be bold, be curious, be intrigued, and investigate. This is your way of demonstrating from the very beginning that you are invested, interested, and willing to do what it takes to do the best job you can. Think of yourself as an investigator on the hunt for how to get this client and your job is to get all the valuable information you can and piece it together to create a powerful outcome.

Be cautious not to get too attached to the information you gather. Be sure to double and cross check it. Find patterns that are overlapping and allow your intuition to guide you. Your intuition is your unconscious, processing information in greater detail than you could ever consciously do on your own. Remaining neutral in the information gathering process allows your unconscious to sort and sift through the material more efficiently and gives you a clearer instinct about how to proceed through the conversation.

Also by allowing yourself to remain relatively indifferent you have the ability to show up in the moment, to be flexible enough to influence from where the prospect is rather than where you assume they are. Remember our job is not to diagnose. Leave that to the medical and psychological community. Our job is to figure out how they are doing what they are doing and to change it to improve and optimize their outcome, whether they are an individual or an organization.

Being attached to what is wrong distracts you from the most valuable information that is right in front of you.

Years ago when I was in a club partying in Bangkok I met a cute looking guy. I approached him with the intention of hitting on him. He knew what I was up to and quickly notified me that I was barking up the wrong tree. He wasn't upset or offended. He explained that this happened to him a lot actually. Rather than run away with my tail between my legs we continued talking about what we both did and became friends.

We eventually met for a complimentary session. Before the session I looked him up on Facebook and noticed that he identified as an "atheist." I later found out that he was so atheist that he would give the atheist handbook out as Christmas gifts. I gathered from this that none of my usual spiritual vocabulary would go over very well with him. So I made note of it and I tested it during the complimentary session. I asked him what his thoughts were about life after Earth. His response confirmed my intuition about avoiding language like higher-self, spiritual being, non-physical, angels, guides, and so on.

I decided to keep the conversation direct, scientific in nature, and process driven. I spoke in his language and explained the concepts as I felt he would best understand them from his map of the world. It is important that we take the information we gather before meeting for the complimentary session and begin to map out their world and also not come to solid conclusions until we can confirm that they think the way they do.

Each person has a unique way of thinking about their life experience. They have their own map of world and way of processing information. Our job is to understand that as much as we can and, for brief moments, to step as fully into that world as we can. By doing so we are able to influence them in ways they are not even able to do for themselves. This is why we are such a valuable asset to others.

What is your pre-game ritual?

It is important to be sure that you are in the proper state before heading into your complimentary session. There is a lot on the line. It is important that you are at your very best. In order to do so it is important to create a ritual before your meetings, including regular sessions with clients. Some suggestions would be to do some nice deep breathing. Get relaxed and calm. Think of times in the past where things went smoothly for you and you were in a flow state. Create a mantra or incantation and repeat it out loud, looking in the mirror, and you may even want to add some physical movement to get your physiology involved further activating the state.

What matters is that you have a specific series of steps that involve all the systems--visual, auditory, and kinesthetic--that when activated puts you into a powerful state ready to take on the task at hand. Almost every professional athlete has a pre-game ritual. You may even have one that you're not even consciously aware of and what you can do now is create one. Ask others about their pre-game ritual; try it on, if it works keep it or make it even better. Having mastery over your emotional state will increase your chances of success and this is the way to do it. Check everything else at the door and take on the mindset of success through your thoughts and it will flow through your feelings and as a result your words, actions, and behavior will reflect it on the outside beautifully and be infectious to those that come into contact with you.

THE COMPLIMENTARY SESSION AKA THE SALES CALL

"If you go out looking for friends, you're going to find they are very scarce. If you go out to be a friend, you'll find them everywhere."

— Zig Ziglar

As we go through the different aspects of the complimentary session it may seem as though they are linear steps. This is only true from a general perspective. The truth is the complimentary session is a combination of sequential steps and multi-dimensional ones that are happening together at the same time. For the purpose of explanation, I am going to outline them here sequentially. Your job is to keep in mind that while you are learning a general process here in a series of steps, many of the components we will go through are happening at the same time. So, whether you are doing several things at once, or putting them together in a series, eventually the end of this chain of agreements, which we discussed earlier, is them hiring and paying you.

Here are the General Steps of the Selling Process

>Build Rapport
>Gather Information
>Present Opportunity
>Handle Objections
>Close
>Future Pace
>Ask for Referrals

Rapport is a natural positive side effect of a variety of things. Seeking to understand the person you are interacting with and demonstrating you understand them is the most powerful way that I've found. There are endless resources about rapport, so much so, that the consumer has become aware of many of these tactics and there is no need to waste time here elaborating on common rapport building methods.

In short, the goal of creating rapport is that the prospect feels understood, comfortable, that they trust you, feel that you are like them, and that you have their best interest at heart. I've found that some of this is more important than others. Gaining a high level of rapport can certainly make selling easier. When you take the time to discover how the prospect thinks and model that back to them, rapport happens automatically and it happens unconsciously which is our goal in influencing others.

Gathering Information

The gathering information step has already begun before the complimentary session. It began the moment they came into your awareness. This is the investigation step where you are thoroughly gathering information. This, in my opinion, will be an ongoing process throughout your relationship with them. In many ways, you're constantly gathering information about your client. It is the most important and valuable thing you do as a coach because the better you understand them the more precision you will have in influencing them. Are you getting the point yet?

The most effective way to get the information you are seeking is to, you've guessed it, ask precise questions. Your questions will uncover a number of things including how they think of the world, also known as their beliefs, how they identity themselves or their "I AM", their core values, and how they prioritize those values. You also want to understand the specifics of how they think and model their world internally.

People only think in two ways; visually and auditorily. These visual and auditory thoughts create feelings and these feelings operate behavior. Understanding how they represent their reality through visual and auditory representations in their mind is critical to being masterful at influencing them to do things.

You also want to understand how they make decisions, especially "big" decisions, like buying a house, investing their money, buying a car, pursuing a long term relationship, their job, or the business they pursued. What are their big reasons to hire you? What are their big reasons that will stop them from hiring you? Who else is involved in this buying decision? These are very important questions.

If there is someone else responsible in the decision making process you'll want to extend this process out and make sure they are involved in the conversation as soon as possible. If they are available call them into the meeting right away. There is no point in having to go through this twice or worse run the risk of blowing the sale by not having the decision maker in the conversation. If you can't get them involved be sure that before you end the meeting you ask your prospective client to clearly tell you what they intend telling the decision maker. Do not finish the meeting until they are so convinced that they will get the ultimate decision maker to go for it since you can't be there to lead that conversation.

A great question to ask to start this conversation is "What will you tell your (wife, accountant, lawyer, boss, human resources, etc.) when they ask what your reasons are for doing this?" Listen carefully to their response. You'll know if they have the conviction necessary to get the decision maker on board or not. Coach them through it so that they, in their best ability, represent you well in the conversation. It will also tell you if they are actually on board or if they are using this decision maker as an excuse not to work with you rather than being up front about it.

The Big Why, What will motivate them to the core?

Your number one job is to ask the right questions to get you and the prospect to where you want them. The other is to pull out their motivation to do this. We rarely ask why. We usually put it in more agreeable terms like "What are your reasons?" or the like. We want to find out their "Why" and amplify it so big that the motivation saturates them. The "Why" has to become so big that the "How" becomes irrelevant in the decision making process. When your "Why" is big enough you find a way to do what you want.

Think about a time in your life that you had no idea how you were going to do something, yet your determination was so strong that you found a way to do it and you succeeded. This is the key to creating the life you want. Make the "Why" so big that the heavens open and come one way or another you find a way to make it happen.

What are the consequences of them not changing?

Want to know what sells? Pain sells. It's sad but true. The number one motivator, more than 70% of the time, is pain, potential pain, or consequences. Many of the most successful people on the planet are successful because they are primarily motivated away from pain: the fear of failing, the fear of losing out, the pain of not being good enough. Your job, as uncomfortable as it can be for some of you, is to dig up that pain, put a spotlight on it, and present yourself as the solution to it. So how is missing this opportunity going to hurt them? How are you going to help them avoid that?

Asking these questions is not enough to get the information that you need to influence them consciously and more importantly unconsciously. In order for you to get the answers you seek it requires that you are able to listen, observe, and feel the information that they may or may not be telling you directly. Most people aren't even aware themselves of how they think, let alone be able to tell you directly, even when asked. In a sales environment they are even more unlikely to be completely vulnerable with you, even if they are aware, that is until they trust you.

Your job is to ask the right questions and be able to listen to the words they use along with their non-verbal cues to guide them into giving you the information you require. You are an interrogator and an explorer out on the frontier on a search for a very valuable commodity, like oil. Each question is drilling down below the surface and evaluating the results you get. When you get a piece of what you want, then drill down even deeper to get closer to the core of the information vital to influence the person.

It is important to know when to dig deeper and when to move on. There is also the element of the other person. They believe they are involved in a conversation meanwhile you are juggling the many components of the process. They may want to indulge in their story as they tell it and that story could be the very distraction that takes you off the path to getting them to their desired outcome. Your job is to keep you both on track, drilling down into the powerful content that is going to clearly answer the questions from above and maintaining rapport. The key is knowing when you've got what you need, and then moving on, politely and directly.

This can be tricky because you'll have complimentary sessions where the prospect will be all over the place or dominate the conversation. There is a delicate balance between taking the lead and inadvertently offending your prospect. You have a very limited amount of time to do what you need to do to get them to buy and you also need to be respectful of them and their story. This is one of the many reasons practicing is so important. The more people you play this out with the more powerful you will become in your ability to do this smoothly.

I use the following language patterns when redirecting clients "Could we pause there for just a moment (and go back to) or (could you tell me about_____)." "I want to make sure I understand something that isn't clear to me, tell me more about _____ ." "Wait just a moment, tell me about _____."

Something we all share is we have a unique experience of reality. Meaning there is the true experience and then there is the individual's reality of that experience. Think about when a friend was telling a story about an experience that you both shared and their account of the experience had major differences in the story line from your memory. Are they wrong? Maybe, in some cases. What I'm suggesting is that they aren't wrong per se, rather they are relaying their "reality" of the situation. What is true to them is not necessarily true to you, and yet you were together in the same "experience."

In order for us to remain relatively sane and to move through life our neurological system is required to filter out information. There are millions upon millions of bits of data coming into one's neurological system over a lifetime. The conscious mind can only focus on 7 +/- 2 things (or 3-7 things) at any given time. The unconscious can focus on many, many times more, and yet even it has to sort out relevant and irrelevant information. The process through which it does this is through a system of filtering information. These filters have been set up as a result of one's life experience.

Somewhere along the line, the individual and their brain decided what information was important and in which contexts. When meeting people it is important to remove judgment from this process of understanding. Judgment inhibits one's ability to enter the world of the other person and limits one's ability to influence the person they are judging. As you get better at gathering information you will be able to quickly discern how one filters information and under what context.

When working with a successful businessman I discovered that in the context of his business he was very good at clearly identifying where he wanted his business to go. He stated his goals and targets in the positive and outlined the steps very clearly. He knew exactly what he wanted, the kind of people he wanted to serve, the service he provided, how his company would provide it, and the kind of people he wanted working for him. When I asked him about finding the love of his life, however, his filter quickly switched from what he wanted to what he wanted to avoid. This was a stark contrast in how he thought about his business. He was very successful in business and had, up to this point in his life, not created a successful romantic relationship.

It is important to understand that when creating the life that you want you need to know what having a good life means. Taking the time to clearly identify it, and stating it in the positive, gives you a clear target to start moving towards. If I asked you to shoot a gun and hit the target in front of you, your chances of doing so are phenomenally higher than if I only tell you what to avoid hitting. When you are motivated primarily away from consequences, you are backing away from things in life and the chances of you getting what you want drop significantly, and you are more likely to back away into something equally as bad or even worse.

During the complimentary session your job is to first understand whether your prospective client moves towards the things they want or backs away from the possible consequences of what they don't want, and in what contexts they do each. Your job isn't to change them, not yet. You will teach them how to think and do things differently to improve their experience after they hire you. Your job is to understand them, model that understanding and demonstrate you understand them, walk in their world, and to motivate them as they are in the moment so that they hire you.

The atheist I discussed before listened to me because I stepped into his world. I used his language and described things as he understood them in the moment. He felt unconsciously that I understood him because I took the time and cared enough to walk in his world along his side rather than trying to convert him to mine.

People feel connected to us when they believe we are like them. Not once did I compromise myself or break integrity. I didn't pretend to be an atheist, actually, quite the contrary. What I did do was I talked like him, breathed like him, found out how he thinks, and then led him through his own thinking to motivate him to work with me.

He did end up hiring me. I used powerful techniques to focus his mind, remove limiting beliefs, install new resourceful beliefs, and opened his heart to his heart's desire and soul's journey in spite of him not believing in any of it. Months later after seemingly miraculous results showed up in the manifestation of his experience I explained to him what we had done. I used my words from my map of the world. I could do that because by this point we had created a relationship and a bond of trust so that he felt more than comfortable to walk in my world. Though it was never my intention, he no longer identifies as an atheist or gives out atheist handbooks for Christmas. We joke now about how limited and rigid his thinking *used* to be. Not to mention how much better his life and business are as a result of the work he did.

We are NOT the messiah nor is it our job to convert others into what we think is best. Our job is to understand them, the entirety of them, the light and the dark, the lovable and the unlovable. We are here to accept them as they are and recognize that they are whole and perfect in all their imperfections, just as we accept and love ourselves. From this place we are here to assist them to do things more intelligently, with more conscious thinking, and change the habitual unconscious thinking that keeps them from getting what they want. Ultimately the laws that govern this Universe are always operating whether one believes in or understands them. When the student is ready the laws will reveal themselves in due time. It is inevitable. That part of the process is not our job; rather, it can be a positive side effect.

There are a variety of filters of how people think. We've discussed one one already; how they are motivated. All human behavior is motivated in two ways; towards the good stuff or away from the bad stuff. I've had countless coaches spiral into long winded discussions about whether or not this is accurate which is a huge waste of time. Each and every discussion, 100% of the time, has been ended with this remaining true. Yes, each situation and decision is unique, as is the strategy that got them there. But, alas the core of the motivation, in any situation, is one of these two, or a combination thereof.

Knowing this is incredibly valuable information. Knowing how the person you are wanting to influence does it, and in what context, is even more powerful. A client referred me to a moderately successful business owner that was blocked on how to get his business to the next level. In our discussion it became profoundly clear that he was motivated primarily away from negative consequences. Extreme polarity to one end of the spectrum is less common. More often it is a combination of the two, with the prospect being weighted more one direction than the other.

In this client's case he was a very away from the bad stuff kind of guy. A lot of people get frustrated in this kind of conversation because it may feel like no matter what you say to the guy, he has some negative response. Think of any difficult case like this as an "If you can't beat 'em, join 'em" opportunity. What I'm really suggesting is that you just go ahead and skip the attempting to "beat 'em" part and go directly into the "join 'em" all the while maintaining integrity and avoiding compromising yourself. What I'm saying throughout this chapter is just "join 'em." Meet them where they are and lead them to where you want them to be.

This particular client, the polarity responder, also made the majority of his decisions internally, meaning he didn't rely much on other people's opinions or external information. Actually in a lot of cases, if he was given a suggestion by someone, he would act in opposition to the suggestion. It was as if there was some button in his brain that when pressed would respond counter to whatever pushed it. Rather than push hard on that button, like most people do in this case, I decided to use it to my benefit.

In discussing our work together, I didn't present many benefits. I talked more about the negative consequences of us not working together. I didn't directly present them either. Rather, I asked him questions that led him to say them. I asked him where he would be in five years if things went on the way they were. What were the worst case scenarios and how would that affect him? I didn't make suggestions, and I didn't talk about how it would affect the people around him. The more he talked, the more he felt like he had to work with me, and that otherwise this terrible life would be his only choice. And when it came time to close I said to him "You are the only person that knows whether or not we should work together," to which he replied "Let's do it."

Most people in this situation would go crazy dealing with someone like this. I decided to go about it the easy way. I didn't flinch at his overt negative attitude. I didn't judge him. When you suspend judgment and criticism and seek to understand you take the path of least resistance. This is how he filtered information and this is the world I had to walk in. These kinds of interactions become an opportunity to exercise flexibility and neuroplasticity. The person with the most flexibility wins every time. When you are able to chameleon and shape shift into other people's reality you are able to impact them in ways you never imagined possible.

Kids are the best example of this. There are kids that don't ever flinch when they go after what they want. If they want that candy bar in the store, they will throw themselves on the ground and wail until they get it. How many times have you heard a kid ask for something, be told no, and moments later they asked again and keep asking until they get what they want? They are relentless. This is flexibility.

Years ago when I was doing my sales training in finance I was about to close a sale. My mentor at the time asked how certain I was that we were going to close. I was totally certain. He asked me to do an experiment. He said he wanted me to push so hard that I would lose the sale and get myself kicked out of the meeting. I thought he was insane, and looking back at it, he probably was. I did as he instructed. They agreed to proceed. They signed the paperwork, wrote the check and put it on the table. So the experiment began. I broke protocol. I started talking about all kinds of future planning and pushing it hard. The clients were confused and irritated. So much so they picked their check up and told me they were no longer comfortable working with me and would I please see myself out.

As whacky as this experiment was, it taught me some valuable lessons. Number one, maybe it is better to just play out a scenario in your mind than to actually do it, but I would never change anything I've done in my life because it has such rich resources in it. What I really learned was how far I thought I was able to go and tested the limits. It taught me when to push and when to be gentle. It taught me rules, boundaries, and limitations. It taught me to be more flexible. Even though I didn't get paid that day, I learned things that have earned me many times over the money I lost. I eventually called those clients and apologized to them and gained back their trust, which to me is a testament to how much resilience a relationship can have professionally or personally when you are authentic, have integrity, and love what you do. You can screw it up and still be friends.

Back to Mr. Negative. Immediately after he hired me I taught him to start thinking of things he wanted to do and understand that by stating them in the positive he was considerably more likely to achieve them. I installed new ways of thinking that allowed him to take into consideration external influences like the opinions and thoughts of others when navigating life. This all came after he signed with me to be a client, not during the complimentary session. If I would have attempted that during the complimentary session, it would have likely cost me the sale.

Here is a list of filters people use when navigating their world. This is not a comprehensive list of all of them. These are the ones that I believe will be most helpful for you to identify when selling to a prospective client. Remember, extremes of these filters, in most cases are less common. More common is a blend or landing somewhere on the spectrum. What is important is that you identify first where they are on this spectrum, and second in what *context*.

Common Filters for the purpose of our discussion

    Towards or Away
    Proactive or Reactive
    Internal or External
    General or Details
    Visual, Auditory, and Kinesthetic
    Convincer Strategy
    Options or Procedures
    Sameness or Difference

The following brief explanations will help you understand how the other common filters function and questions and ideas to discover them about your prospective client.

Towards or Away

Is this person motivated by the opportunity and pleasurable outcome (toward) or by the possible pain and consequences (away)?

A great question to ask is what would you expect to get out of this if you were to do it? This question does not lead them to answer you specifically about the benefits or the potential consequences they may be avoiding. It leads them to expose it to you naturally as they answer. If you ask "What will you get out of this that is good for you?" You are focusing them consciously on giving you the potential pleasure.

Asking neutral questions throughout this process is very important. Once you begin to notice the pattern, use it in your language in your discussion with them. Remember the majority of people are motivated away from pain and in many cases it's a blend of the two. Be precise and direct them. A great question when you want to tip them over the edge is "What are the consequences of this not changing?" It rings the dinner bell and gets them to the table. Be eloquent when and how you use this question. Experiment, test, and practice, practice, practice.

Proactive or Reactive

Do they take the time to consider and plan their decision (proactive) or do they just respond to the opportunity to make a decision (reactive)?

For example if they are a first responder on an medical emergency team it is highly likely that it is best for them to be reactive. Meaning they don't respond with deep consideration and thought. They handle the situation.

If they are at the helm of a multi-national corporation it is more important they are proactive. Meaning they take time and deep consideration before making changes in a system that involves hundreds of thousands of people and high levels of logistics.

In Stephen Covey's book "7 Habits of Effective People" he writes at length about the power and the importance of being proactive rather than reactive when it comes to success. This is a generalization and for the most in our culture I agree with what Covey suggests. People are far too reactive as a habit and this inhibits their opportunities. Again the power of being in a state of awareness is that you can now use your super power ability to be both Proactive and Reactive when it best suits the environment, situation, and in what context. Again flexibility over being hard wired.

Internal or External

The client I discussed above was primarily internal. Meaning he made decisions usually without outside influence. The way I came to this conclusion is because when I asked him how he made other big decisions in his life he said that he "just knew." I dug deeper and asked who he relied on to come to that decision. Was his wife, parents, mentors, or advisors? All was a no. He did the things he did because he knew inside it was the right thing to do. To his credit this served him very well in many aspects of his life. In others it was creating a disaster.

On the other end of the spectrum is the external. This person can barely function without outside influence in the form of other people and/or facts and figures. They have to inquire if they should go pee or not. They can't even consider the idea of taking action and making a decision on their own instincts. These are sad cases and make for a very limited life. There are as many opinions about what you should or shouldn't be doing in as many contexts as there are combinations of such thus making for an infinite number of potential outcomes. This creates a life that is pulled in all kinds of directions and never really activates the soul and the heart's desire to fulfill its purpose.

> Most people are a combination and follow a sequence based on the context they are making a decision about.
>
> Internal- this person knows within self
>
> Internal with external check- knows within self and checks in with external source to make final decision
>
> External- told by others and/or relays on facts and figures
>
> External with internal check- told by others, facts and figures, and makes decision after confirming internally

There is no right or wrong way of sorting and filtering, rather an optimal way in relationship to any given context. For example you may know with your everything that the Sushi restaurant down the street is where you want to eat dinner with your new potential in-laws. Though it could greatly benefit you to check with your significant other first. What if your new Mom and Dad hate seafood or worse have a severe allergy to it?

General or Details

Some of us prefer to work from the general or broad view. We like to hold a visionary position and orchestrate things. We are able to create systems and organize large intricate things because we are far enough above them to get the bird's eye view required for creating master plans and systems. Once these systems are created though, we are usually the least qualified to follow through and implement them.

Then there are those of us who love the nitty-gritty details. We know every finite detail and follow it precisely. These details are what drive us. Knowing them and keeping them organized gives us a thrill. We can follow the system to a T, but it is unlikely that we created it.

These are descriptions of the extremes of this sorting pattern. My greatest growth personally was learning how to not only be the visionary, general perceiver, but also to be detailed when it was the sorting pattern that best served me in my experience, and I learned to enjoy it.

That came while I was in finance. You can throw together a master financial plan, but without the details of how it all works you don't really know the short, medium, and long term results and consequences of those decisions.

Personal power is not only being one or the other, but being able to move into and out of the particular sorting pattern that best serves the experience you are having at the moment.

I'm by no means the most detailed oriented person on the planet, though I am more than ever, while still being able to envision the future of my life and our company.

Visual, Auditory, and Kinesthetic

When asking about this sorting pattern be sure to avoid using sensory words like look, sound, imagine, feel, taste, hear, listen, watch etc. Use general questions like "How do you think about that?"

People will use sensory words in their language all the time to tell you exactly how they think. When you listen you'll notice which ones they use the most. Also it will come out in their communicative behavior. A ***Visual*** person usually talks faster. They are racing to get the words out before the pictures go away. An ***Auditory*** person is more likely to speak with annunciation, pronouncing words, and using a detailed vocabulary. How their words sound and their communication is very important. A person who prefers the ***Kinesthetic*** will often be slow to respond as they are processing through their feelings, will speak slowly, and will often leave out much of the details.

Think about yourself for a moment and what sense do you prefer the most? You may have an idea of which sensory system you prefer or you may relate more to one of the descriptions above. Knowing who you've been for a long time can be useful. It is most useful when you use this information to know where to grow as a person and a source of influencing others. Knowing what kind of person your prospect is, becomes even more useful in the context of the complimentary session. When you enter their world and speak from this sensory system, they will feel unconsciously that you are like them, that you understand them, and that they trust you and are comfortable enough to buy from you.

How are they convinced?

In order to understand how someone is convinced ask a series of questions in the context of what you want to convince them to have, do, or be. Here is an example:

Question 1:

How do you know that your [child is a good student]?

Pay close attention to the how they reply. Remember what sense (visual, auditory, and kinesthetic) they prefer is also a sorting pattern. They will expose this preferred sort to the context in the language they use. "I have to see them doing their homework." (Visual) or "I talk to their teacher about it." (Auditory) or "I feel when they do they homework they are a good student." (Kinesthetic)

Question 2:

How many times do you have to (see, hear, read, do) that to be convinced [they are a good student]?

They will answer conversationally in one of the following sorting pattern. Listen closely as they tell you their personal story of how they are convinced and listen for the patterns and filters.

-A number of times
-Automatically
-Consistently
-Over a period of time

Based on their response and the context in which you ask the question you will know how they were convinced. If you ask enough questions you can figure out how someone thinks and in turn reflect their thinking back to them so that they feel, on a very deep level, that you understand them. This also gives you the equation for how to present information so that they will assimilate it better because you are presenting to how their mind thinks.

Options or Procedures

This sorting pattern is important to know about your client because it can be one of the easiest ways to influence your prospect. The reason I say that is because it will give you the exact road to take them down. For example, an options person wants to know what choices they have to make a decision. Therefore when you present the opportunity (aka do the sales pitch) you can give them a number of options and they will choose from one of them. Of course, not working with you isn't an option, that is, as long as you want them as your client.

Procedure people love compliance and protocol. When presenting the opportunity tell them how it works, the steps, the procedure, and map it out for them so they understand that this path leads to one place, working with you. The majority of the population are procedure people. Without it, they feel confused, scared, lost, and like they can't feel certain about their experience and what to expect. It is a good idea to know which of the two types you are talking to and speak to that directly. This will make your job a whole lot easier.

Sameness or Difference

Questions to discover this sorting pattern:

Q: What is the relationship between _____ and _____?

Ex: What is the relationship between this year and last year?

It is important to keep the questions throughout this process neutral and to avoid leading them to a specific sort. Listen to their language. Are they talking about how things are the same or how they are different? Is it a combination? If so how is it weighted and in what order. Read the sorting patterns below and think about where they fit in.

Sameness- same no change

Sameness with Exception- more, better, comparisons

Difference- change, new, unique, variety

Sameness with Exception and Difference- new and comparisons

The reason this is important is because you want to know how to present your opportunity. Are they looking for how this opportunity is like things they know or different from them? People who look for the sameness in things want everything to be the same and you want to be the same as good decisions they've made in the past: Things that worked out well and over the long term the more they think about them the better they feel.

The difference person on the other hand will want to know how this is different from other coaching opportunities. They are really good at dissecting the differences. Remember those games when you were a kid when you have two pictures and you have to find the differences? These people are really good at those puzzles. How would you talk to someone that you know is looking for the differences and how can you leverage that to get them to buy form you and change over time. It can be a valuable asset to be a difference person in some areas of their life and it can be a curse.

Our job is to talk to these people wherever they are on this spectrum and to influence them to keep doing what they do well or even improve upon it and eventually change the focus in other areas. Personal power is flexibility. Master focusing these filters where they are best suited, and you will experience freedom you never imagined.

Personal power is being able to move into and out of these preferred ways of thinking and into the one that is most optimal given the situation, environment, or context in which you are operating and to the person you are influencing.

This is called flexibility. Master flexibility and all matters of your life and work will go with more ease and in a natural flow. Knowing you are a detail person is great. Growing and adapting so you are able to change your focus into the details and out to the broad general (and enjoy it) is a very profound skill. We call this freedom. Knowing you are visual is pretty cool. Being able to activate your auditory and kinesthetic systems fully as well, is the ultimate power. This is where intelligence, greatness, and genius come from. Being able to activate all the senses and move fully into your mind in ways that best fit the experience you are in at the moment is personal power and the ultimate freedom. This is profound. Especially when walking in someone else's world.

If you have a detail person and you prefer the general experience, guess what, you roll up your sleeves and get down into the details. It may be difficult at first. Similar to a kid learning to ride a bike with no training wheels. Challenging? Yes. Will you screw it up at first? Yes. Possible? Yes. And over time with determination and practice you will get very, very good. I wonder what other ways your experience will improve by you becoming more adaptable and flexible?

The most successful sales people and influencers on the planet all share in common their ability to create relationships.

My definition of healthy relationships are the outcome of a bond of familiarity based on what you have in common, trust, and experience over time all the while maintaining continuity in integrity, consistency, and not compromising oneself.

In a very short amount of time you will create the feeling of this with your prospective client and you'll do it primarily unconsciously. Unconsciously you want them to feel they like you, that you are like them, that you understand them, and that you have their best interest at heart. They can consciously get that, but it is their unconscious that will give them the feeling that will motivate them to work with you.

I recommend when meeting a prospective client for the first time that you spend half of the time or more gathering information. The better you understand them, how they think, what drives them, motivates them, and what is at stake the more effective you'll be when it comes time to give them the sales pitch. Mastering this process is the difference between making a fortune and getting by in our industry. Also the better you know them, the better you know if this is a relationship worth pursuing from your end. Remember that every sales call ends with a close. The question is will you close *them* to hire you? or Will they close *you* to not work together?

Presenting the Opportunity

At some point in this process you're going to want to actually present your opportunity to the prospective client; this is also known as the "sales pitch." Be clear, be concise, and use all that valuable information that you gained throughout the information gathering part of the process.

Many sales people have their "schtick" which is defined as a gimmick, comic routine, style of performance. This is what they say and how they say it, almost every time. Every time? Yes, almost every time. Don't be that person. If you are, please throw this book away, or give it to someone who can benefit from it. Although you shouldn't have a set schtick, it is a good idea to have a clear plan of how to explain what you do, how you do it, pricing, timeline, and the details about how this is all going to work out. Know your pitch inside and out and how to present it to a variety of type of people. Prepare stories and metaphors to fit into the different maps of the many worlds people live in. Then, in the moment, customize it to the person you are speaking to, based on what you just learned about them while you were gathering information.

If they like avoiding consequences and don't believe in God, then avoid God and things of a spiritual nature and talk about the pain and suffering they are going to avoid as a result of the coaching process. If they love details, then by all means get down and dirty with the details, inundate them. The magical name for this process is called thinking. Comprehend what you are learning about them, and use it when you present to them. They'll appreciate it, mostly unconsciously, which is what really matters any way.

Granted what you do and how you do it, in general terms, is the same for all of your clients. Your fee is your fee. What is different is how you present it. You want to present it while standing with them in their world. Use their language, their beliefs, and their perspective all the while installing in them your conviction, determination, and certainty about how right the decision to work with you is and will be.

Handling Objections

For most sales people objections are their worst nightmare. They wish they had a magic wand to dissolve them away. Objections, however, are a natural part of the selling process and they will inevitably rear their ugly heads. Being masterful in handling them is one of the most powerful skills of influence you can possess, one that will multiply your income many times and get the most difficult deals to go through.

First things, first: I would like to turn this "detesting of objections" idea on its head. Since objections are inevitably going to come up, I suggest we get excited when our customer or client objects. The reason I suggest this is because an objection is a clear indicator that the close is more likely to happen than ever before in the conversation. Objections create the greatest opportunity to close.

Let me say that again: Objections create the greatest opportunity to close.

You already know that there are certain inherent objections that come with your product or service. They are built in and you get them all the time. Things like "it costs too much" or "I don't think I can get what I need out of it." List these classic objections you commonly get and start to clear them away in the conversation with your prospects long before they have the opportunity to bring them up. For example if you hear the "costs too much objection" often enough, then it's time to start bringing it up first. Like Barney Fife used to say "Nip it in the bud."

You may want to start explaining the reasons for the greater expense early on and perhaps call it an investment rather than a big ticket item. You may even want to brag about it to your prospects adding greater significance to their investment level. Create a new meaning and handle the objection while it is small and approachable. Handling it before the prospect brings it up, neutralizes it and diminishes the power it has in the decision making process.

There are objections that prospects bring up that actually matter and then there are objections that prospects bring up that don't, but they bring them up because they feel obligated to because that's part of their *buying pattern*. Sometimes the best thing to do is ignore the objection. Walk around it and move the ball down the field in spite of it. If the prospect is determined that this objection matters then let the prospect run with it, perhaps to the point they talk themselves out of it and run out of steam. And, if it really matters to them, that's a really good sign. Pick your battles wisely.

If an objection really matters to a prospect this is good because this objection is the single thing standing between them buying and you selling. This is the moment when you get to feel eager, curious, and even excited. Because once you handle this break point objection you get to close. The best thing to do in this scenario is to get your prospect to agree that this is indeed the final objection. And if not, then ask them what is really keeping them from buying. Many times prospects will tell you the exact final objection, and when they do you're 90% closer to closing the deal.

When you discover what the final objection is, the most important thing to do is to align with the client. Demonstrate you understand their concern and you're on their side by saying so. Use language like "I understand…" "I can appreciate…" "I respect…" or even "I agree…" This way the objection brings you closer to them rather than becoming a potential wedge between you. Stay on their side of the table and be their friend. Remember you are establishing a relationship that will last years and that is always more important than being right.

Next, turn the objection into a question. The reason you want to do this is because you can't answer an objection, but you can answer a question. "It costs too much!" becomes, "I agree, this is a significant investment. Didn't you mention that quality was most important and you believe that you get what you pay for?"

Answering the question and getting the prospect to align with you dissolves the objection. There are, of course, a wide variety of ways for how you do this. That's your job to figure out because it will be specific to the product or service you provide and how the potential customer you're talking to thinks.

There is no cookie cutter approach to how to transform this final objection into a closed client, but now you have a model that will work time and time again as you mold it into place to meet your client where they are and take them to where you want them to go. Ultimately they want to buy from you because of your conviction to stay focused on the target and your willingness to eloquently guide them to be with you. This is the difference between a sales person and a sales professional.

Closing

At some point in the conversation it is going to be blazingly obvious your prospect is ready to become a client. For example you may ask "If we do this, in your opinion which way will be easiest way for you to make payment? Do you think it may be easier to do a wire transfer, write a check, or use a card?" to which they reply "Oh, I'm going to make a transfer from savings to checking and then you can just run my debit card if that works?"

It doesn't get much more obvious than that. And when this moment happens a bell needs to go off in your head. Make it sound like the bell that closes the New York Stock Exchange. Many sales people get the sale faster than they think, and rather than closing the deal, they continue their process. It is as if the prospect says "Ok, I'll buy" and the sales person says "I'm sorry sir/madam I haven't finished my sales pitch yet, please wait." How ridiculous, and sadly it happens.

When your customer is ready to buy, be ready to sell and go to the next logical step, close! They don't need to tell you blatantly they are ready to buy you'll know because they are giving you all the signs. Your job is to congratulate them and then tell them what is going to happen next. Explain the coaching agreement and how to make payment. Schedule their first official session and tell them how excited you are to work with them. Yes, it is that easy, and when you do all the preparatory work to get to this point, it ought to be.

Future Pacing

The final step in the complimentary session is to plan on a wonderful future together, and what they are going to get out of working with you, and to ask for referrals. Ask them "What are you going to get out of the next six months of us working together? How is this going to affect your life and work? Who will you become as a result?" Ask these questions, and then close your mouth and listen. Encourage them to share more. This process is called *Future Pacing*.

They won't be driving home and putting your coaching package in their garage, and they won't be able to show it to their friends and family. What you want them to do is to make their decision so real that they will stick to it. It also plants the seeds of desire, right then and there, so you are again moving them toward this new target.

After they finish talking, request that they continue to really consider these questions about what they are going to get and who they will become. Tell them to think really deeply about that between now and your first session together because you are going to ask them again when you talk. This signals their unconscious mind to bring up even more resources for them and to make those desires even more real which will make your job even easier in the months ahead. Also, if they are busy thinking about what they are going to get, they will be too busy to consider changing their mind.

Asking for Referrals

Ask them who they know that fits the description of your perfect client and may also be interested in a complimentary session. Even if they are unable to answer that question in the moment, by asking it you are preparing them for when you ask again in the future. You are breaking the ice so when you do ask for referrals again later it is a part of the process rather than some awkward, new conversation.

Condition your clients to give you referrals and install the expectation for them early on. This makes it easier. A warm referral is worth ten network marketing meetings or more. This is the most effective way to build your practice quickly. After your practice matures, your income will become steady because of clients sending you new business. In the beginning asking for referrals is how you build the foundation of this momentum.

The more you ask for referrals, the better you will get at it. Remember, everything you are doing takes practice. Practice is the mother of all skill. The more you do it, the easier it becomes and the more comfortable you will do it. Wonder where your next client is? Your current clients, friends, family, and business associates know where they are, recruit them into your marketing plan. I suggest you talk about referrals as part of your pitch. Just drop it in when you are talking about potential results. Think of it as planting a seed that is going to grow and you'll harvest later.

Transferring Conviction

What you are really selling are feelings. Buyers buy when the feeling is right. I like to call it the "sweet spot." That sweet moment when the prospect becomes the buyer and the sales person gets to ring the sales bell. They buy because it feels right. This is true 100% of the time. Not 99.9% or 80%, that's right 100% of the time. This has been neurologically proven. Whether it is buying, or any other activity with a beginning and an end, a person will only make a final decision when they get that good feeling. It's your job to get them there.

Now, are these good feelings always an accurate reading of reality? No, it is not always the most optimal time to buy, the right person to buy from, or the best terms yet buyers make these mistakes all of the time because they get a feeling that it is. That's why integrity is so important in what we do as sales people. It is also why some sales people are perceived as manipulative liars who cheat people. These unscrupulous sales people know how to get people to the good feeling state to buy without doing what is right for them.

Your job, as an integrity driven sales person, is to understand your prospect and how they think in the context of buying your product or service. Then you take this understanding and mirror it back to the prospect. By demonstrating that you understand them, they feel comfortable and at ease to buy from you.

The foundation of a successful sales relationship is in your client or customer feeling understood by you. It doesn't really matter whether you agree with how they think. What is important is that you understand how they think and convey that in your communication. We do not sell products and services. We transfer feelings: Good feelings about our product and service and the customer or client buying them.

When you understand your buyer, you can take them from how they are feeling at the beginning of the process and lead them to climb an emotional ladder to get them to the feeling state *THEY* require to buy.

All of this takes incredible flexibility on your part. You have to be flexible enough to bend and mold yourself into their world, to be like them so much that you can lead them to where you want them to be in order to buy from you. You saturate them with this emotional state on such a level that price isn't the only, or most important, determining factor. Because when you connect so deeply with your prospect they become your friend, and they want their friend to succeed and get the sale more than some sales person down the street who might give them a slightly better price.

Creating a lasting relationship with your customer or client is the most important part of the selling process. When that is your target, along with integrity and doing what is right, you create a professional business rather than a sales job.

As you can tell there is a lot to this single meeting—as there should be. This meeting is the opportunity you have to demonstrate how good you are at getting to know them and at creating a relationship. You get to demonstrate your stability, your ability to influence, and your ability to adapt to the moment, all the while constructing a plan to get them to decide to work with you.

In the beginning this process may take you more than one meeting. I used to do a complimentary session and a follow up. These days I typically open and close a prospective client in forty two minutes and I do so 80% of the time. Additionally my fees exceed far above the national average for professional coaches. How? By doing what I've outlined in this chapter and doing it with precision. It is the side effect of thousands of hours of practice. Rome wasn't built in a day and neither will be your coaching practice.

Do not make the mistake of comparing yourself to me or anyone else on the planet. What is important is that you are learning, growing, and practicing, and as a result getting better and improving all the time. I've heard coaches say to me that they want to be as good as me some day. Though my ego loves the compliment my heart of heart tells these eager souls to strive for a goal worth striving for and that is to be better than you were the day before. When you make that your goal, not only is it stated in the positive, is achievable, and is within your control, it also creates a compounding effect on that target over time. And the result? Manifestation of the most successful version of you!

ALIGN, PLAN, IMPLEMENT, AND MEASURE

"Movement is life. Life is a process. Improve the quality of the process and you improve the quality of life itself."

— Moshe Feldenkrais

As I mentioned in the last chapter, when I started coaching I didn't have any coaching credentials or education. What I did have was a life of experience of having gone from failure to freedom both emotionally and financially. The question on my mind was how did I do it? How did I become this person so far removed from my origins as a consciousness?

After some brainstorming, and many pages of mapping it out, this is what I created. The system is general in nature, because each person that shows up in your practice is already on their journey in full motion. Your intersection with them is the moment where the course of this journey changes forever. This system is the platform and they are the engine that will propel it. They are also the driver. They are at the wheel. They are responsible for where they take themselves and for their successes and failures.

Your job is to guide. You are to walk next to them, or to use the earlier metaphor, you will be their temporary co-pilot and navigator for this moment in their experience. It is important that you view your position as an equal to them. There is no rank or caste. Just two souls coming together on this journey for a moment to bring about more fun, amplify both of your heart's desires, create growth and expansion.

Once your client has paid and signed your coaching agreement the next step is to have an introductory session. During this session we introduce daily activities that they will complete for the next forty days consecutively. The reason why they do this forty day challenge is because the daily activities are going to get them to think differently, affect their energy, and get them into alignment more of the time. It also installs these daily activities and makes them more habitual. They are more likely to be successful by doing them for this period of time.

Here is a list of the daily activities to create alignment:

>   Incantations & Mantras
>   Alkalizing
>   Deep breathing to center
>   Meditate for 15-20 minutes
>   Daily Exercise for 30-90 minutes
>   Journaling about their experience
>   Writing 10 or more things that they appreciate
>   Write 5 Powerful Questions

Incantations & Mantras

Whether you are aware of it or not, you talk to yourself a lot and so do your clients. In many cases a lot of what we say isn't very meaningful and productive. The people who are the meanest to us most of the time are ourselves. It is sad, but true. What you say to yourself and how you say it has a massive impact on your life, health, relationships, the amount of money you earn, and how you earn it. This internal dialogue has a huge impact on everything in your experience. This is why taking control of that internal dialogue is so powerful, and is such an important daily activity.

Your first job is to begin to listen to yourself, really listen. At first just let it rip, don't attempt to censor it or change it. Pretend you are the NSA and your job is to investigate your self-talk. When are you kind, supportive, and your biggest cheerleader? When are you mean, abusive, and destructive to yourself? It is important to become aware of it so that you can begin to change it. Most of what we do slips under our radar because it is unconscious; these are habituated and conditioned responses. We don't think, we remember.

Think about what you want to create in your life and what you need to think and feel in order to get there. Begin to craft a personal empowerment statement. This statement is to be written stated in the positive and in the present tense. Use the words I AM to activate your identifying the statement as true. Here is my personal empowerment regarding coaching:

"*I, Dustin Vice, am a powerful force that draws from the source that I AM to create anything I wish to have, do, or be. I have the ability to influence others to create powerful change to create the life they want, desire, and ultimately deserve. Wealth flows to me easily and freely in abundance because I am one with God and God is all things."*

After you have written your personal empowerment statement begin reciting it in the morning several times. Say it aloud, with feeling and emotion. Make it real. You want your entire nervous system to be singing with the emotion of your message. Every cell of your body will get the message. When you speak to yourself in this way you activate a release of neurotransmitters that flood the bloodstream and they change your experience. The message you send becomes the target of your outcome and the center of your focus.

As you listen to yourself throughout the day, take note of the things you say that are resourceful and to the things that don't feel good. Create mantras, or personal empowerment statements for the things that don't feel good, and when those negative comments come up, say those mantras. Make talking to yourself in a resourceful way a habit. Soothe yourself and give yourself relief. It is difficult enough with outside pressure to make the inside a wonderful place to be. Start your day off by focusing your mind and saturating yourself with good feelings. It will make all the difference.

Alkalizing

Alkalizing consists of consuming of foods and drinks that balance the PH of your body. The majority of things we consume are acidic in nature, which can even include the air that we breathe. Acid in the body creates mucus and inflammation. It also impairs the communication in the neurological system. It is important to counter this by reducing the consumption of acidic food and drinks and increase the intake of things that are alkaline. I like to drink freshly juiced wheat grass, powdered magnesium, kombucha, apple cider vinegar diluted with water, or water mixed with a significant amount of fresh lemon or lime juice. I would suggest researching what food and drinks you can consume to improve the PH balance of your body.

The neurological system is an electric system, meaning it works through the movement of electricity in the system. When your system is PH balanced the conductivity of that system is increased and it communicates better. You experience more energy, clearer thinking, and a calmer mood. When you begin this process you may feel some discomfort because balancing the PH does cause your body to detox.

Though detoxing is healthy some of the side effects can be unpleasant. You may notice your body getting rid of mucus, strange bowel movements, headaches, and fatigue. These are all temporary. Whether detoxing or not, always be sure to drink plenty of water and get plenty of rest especially when first alkalizing. During times of healing and transformation it is very important to get a minimum of eight hours of sleep a day. This is always important and even more so when you are experiencing big changes. This is baseline activity.

It is true that there are a variety of ways you can fast and modify your diet to enhance your well-being. Alkalizing is one of the simplest of these methods, an easy to incorporate practice that will have a powerful impact on your overall alignment.

You should see it as a baseline activity, upon which you may or may not want to add other dietary changes.

Deep Breathing to Center & Meditate for 15-20 minutes

In order to be calm and relaxed your body needs an influx of oxygen. People that are under high levels of stress or anxiety, breathe differently than those that are calm and relaxed. In order to make an intelligent decision and to stimulate the right behavior it requires that we be in a good emotional state. The most powerful and effective way to change your state is by breathing. Breathing deep oxygenates the system and changes your state. In order to meditate, it requires that you relax.

Notice how you are feeling. Just take note and prepare for this to change. If you are already relaxed and calm, then prepare to become even more relaxed now. Breathe in through your nose and imagine your lungs filling up the same way you would fill up a glass with water from a pitcher. Breathe in as deep as possible, for as long as possible. When you reach the deepest inhale, pause for just a moment at the top and then begin slowly exhaling out through the mouth. The goal here is for your exhale to be longer than your inhale, fully emptying your lungs and preparing them for the fresh new oxygen on your next inhale.

If for some reason you have a hard time breathing in through your nose, feel welcome to breathe in through your mouth. What is important is that you are getting as much fresh oxygen into your lungs as possible. If this means breathing in through your mouth that is ok. It is more important that you are breathing deeply than what orifice it comes in and out of, though over time as your lungs develop and become stronger you will be able to breathe properly. It only takes time and practice. Try breathing in through your mouth and out through your nose. Notice how you feel changes, and that you begin to relax more and more.

At the end of each exhale let out a nice, long, deep sigh. Try it now as you are reading this. Deep breath in, hold it for just a short moment, and exhale "Ahhhhhhhhhh." Notice how these deep breaths bring in calm and relaxation. My friend Johnny Otero says "Four deep breaths take you to center." I've had clients do four deep breaths exercise only to tell me that it didn't work. After a little discovery work I found out that it did work, if only for a moment or two and that they were just too worked up to stay centered. If four deep breaths aren't enough for you to maintain this calm, relaxed feeling, then do four more and repeat until your state is totally altered. When you feel good, you know you are in alignment and ready to meditate.

There are many ways to meditate and many things you can do in your meditation. I think generally meditation is way underrated and over hyped. Having the ability to empty your mind is cool but is it really all that productive? I like to use meditation as a time to calm and relax, and also to influence my mind to change and improve. Also to think about things and focus in ways I can't when I'm busy in the world. When we coach we can give our clients assignments to do in their meditations. For our purposes here I will explain our guidelines for beginner meditation.

-Sit upright in a comfortable chair with both feet on the floor and your arms on your lap

-Keep your eyes closed for the entire time you are in meditation

-Stay awake

You may want to set a timer with a soft sound to track how long you are in the meditation. It can be easy to distort time in this state. It is easy to feel like fifteen minutes become hours or that an hour is a few minutes depending on the experience.

In the beginning we consider following the guidelines above as a successful meditation. At first it isn't important where your mind goes or what you think about. Simply sitting in a chair upright, with your eyes closed, while staying awake for fifteen to twenty minutes, is a successful session. For beginners this in itself can be a triumph. These are the goals and over time they become easier.

To enhance the experience you can play soft meditative music, listen to guided meditations, guided trances, practice activities you want to improve or do processes outlined by your coach. What is important is that you and the client begin to practice this process of getting relaxed and calm on purpose daily. The positive side effects of this practice are very powerful. Again, all of these daily activities are starting points. As one develops their meditation practice the goals will change. What is important is starting with goals that are realistic, and that can be done every day for forty days consecutively.

If we could only teach all people how to calm, soothe, and relax themselves more of the time, this world would transform into an unrecognizable experience, from our current perspectives, filled with so much more love and peace. We'll get there, eventually, one person at a time.

Daily Exercise for 30-90 minutes

We (Americans) are the most obese nation on the planet, but don't worry, there are several not far behind us. We have a huge population to compete with, literally. Physical health is the obvious reason why we want to do physical exercise, though there are many other benefits as well. Exercise also creates pain in the muscular system which tells the brain to release oxytocin and other endorphins like serotonin. It make us happier, forces us to breath deeper, and gets the blood flowing. We also detox when we sweat removing a wide variety of toxins. Exercise also creates lactic acid in our bodies which is another reason to alkalize.

I'm not going to do a hard sell on physical exercise. You already know why, so do it, and get your clients to do it as well. The body is the temple for your spirit. Treat it well, and make good use of it, and it will only make your experience better. Getting your clients moving and in their bodies makes a huge impact, especially if they don't usually do it. They will hate you and love you for it. Overall, it is a very smart way to go about helping them.

Journaling, Write Ten or More Things That You Appreciate, & Write Five Powerful Questions

Journaling

There is power in the written word and in documenting your life. This is especially true when going through profound personal change. When you do your job properly as a coach, it will result in profound personal change for your client. It is good for them to process these changes through journaling. They should write out how they are feeling, what their experience is like, and what they are going through. Even if it is just a few sentences, it is a good habit to get into. Also I use the journal time as a means for them to do homework from our coaching. I often have them document any assignments I give in their journal. This way they are accomplishing a daily activity and doing their homework at the same time.

Write Ten or More Things That You Appreciate

What keeps us from fully experiencing joy is our lack of appreciation. Appreciation is a habit and a practice. It is not an attitude of gratitude. In order to experience joy in life you must find a deep sense of appreciation as a practice. This appreciation begins with the ordinary and simple things in life. Life is fleeting and time is always escaping us. Do a quick inventory of the children in your life. Maybe your kids if you have them, your friend's kids, wherever they are in your life think back to when they were born and how old they are now.

It is always a wake-up call to think of how fast time goes by when I measure it by the age of the children around me.

For you to experience joy requires that you catalogue and obsess about what you appreciate and how much you appreciate the experience of life. The more you do that the more rich life will become. We start our clients off by cataloguing ten things for which they are thankful and appreciate. The real intent is to get them to be in appreciation as much as possible and more of the time, though it shocks me how difficult it can be for some people to list ten things for forty consecutive days. When I do my morning meditation I list a 100 things that I appreciate. I allow my mind to fly through them and bring them into my awareness. I suggest you do the same. If there is power in ten, then multiply that by ten and experience the joy that comes with it.

Write Five Powerful Questions

I've written at length about the power of questions. Questions drive our thoughts and organize them into focus. If I ask you how your right foot is feeling suddenly you are thinking about your right foot. It is a question and it changed your focus of attention. Not really that powerful in this example but effective to demonstrate my point none-the-less. If you ask someone what they will have for lunch I wouldn't consider that a powerful question either. If you ask them what could they eat that will nourish their body as the temple for their soul, now there is power in your question.

If you ask someone how to create a better relationship with their daughter it certainly does point them into a better direction. A more powerful question is to ask them "what will it take to create an unparalleled bond with your daughter that will last a lifetime?" What is the difference you feel between these two questions?

A powerful question ignites within you a strong emotional response. It tells the unconscious to dig deeper, fires off more of the brain, and motivates behavior. For the purpose of this daily activity do not try to answer the questions, rather only write them out each day. Plant them as seeds in the far recesses of the mind. The unconscious mind is a powerful machine constantly at work while you are awake and sleeping and dreaming. Actually when you are deep asleep it works even harder processing through the millions of bits of information from your experience. Asking it powerful questions and planting them as seeds, allows the unconscious to process the many layers of the question and begins to bring about the multitude of resources to answer it.

The Coaching Process

Alignment

The process through which we take our clients is, from a general view, simple in nature. The first forty days of the relationship along with the 40 days of daily success activities is aimed at getting the client into a state of alignment more of the time. As they consciously do the daily activities your job is to assist them to process through the deep underlying thinking that is holding them back.

Many of the things that limit us aren't that obvious to us. If they were, we would easily change them. Some of the things are very obvious, yet we are limited in being able to change them. Sometimes we know exactly the cause of our problem, and yet we don't know how to get better. Diagnosis can sometimes be the beginning of healing and is rarely if ever the cure. Your job is to understand how they are doing what they are doing to get their current outcome and to assist them to change it to get a better one.

The simplest reason why alignment is so important is because we feel better in an aligned state. When we feel better, we make better choices, and do things more intelligently. Remember what we discussed earlier: the thoughts, which are represented visually and auditorally in the mind, are what generate our feelings, and these feelings are what motivate our behavior. This is why changing how you think, changes your life experience. When you think differently, you feel differently, and your behavior is motivated to change and life changes.

The challenge is how to change this cascade of thousands of mostly unconscious thoughts when we don't even understand how we are thinking them. This is where NLP® comes into play. NLP®, or Neuro-Linguistic Programming®, was created by modeling how successful people think, and from that modeling has come technologies for how to change the underlying thinking that is inspiring feelings and motivating behavior.

The addict knows logically that by continuing to consume their drug of choice they will eventually lose everything, live a horrid, lonely life, and eventually die. Yet they continue to consume the drug. The abusive spouse knows that the day will come when their behavior will no longer be tolerated and they will lose their family and their loved ones or worse commit an act that lands them in prison, yet they continue the behavior.

The question is not why, but rather how. How do they continue the behavior, when they know that this is not healthy for them or the people around them to continue the behavior? The reason why we do the things that we know aren't good for us isn't because we lack the intelligence to understand we shouldn't do them. We do them because deep in our unconscious are automatic programs running a strategy to do them. The strategy, in itself, is perfect and works every time. The coach's primary focus during the alignment period, the first forty days, is to remove these old programs that are holding the client hostage and to install new programs to get them to think differently, feel differently, make better decisions, and to behave differently as a result.

The change happens instantly on a neurological level. Some of the results also come instantly while others come over time. In the moment there is the change and the ability to think differently. If they couldn't ride in an elevator because of a debilitating phobia before and a few minutes after a powerful technique they can get in the elevator calm and relaxed, free of the fear, then that is an instant positive side effect of the change.

The question now is what else can they do that they thought they couldn't or was impossible? How else is this change going to show up in their life? How much more freedom will they have? What else will this affect? The mind is holographic in nature. The change was created in that moment and the ripple effects instantly begin to affect other areas of the mind and as a result their life.

Alignment doesn't end on day forty-one. Alignment is a never ending process. We are constantly moving into, and out of alignment, with our best selves and feeling good. Throughout every day we have moments when we are in the flow and others when we are out. The goal isn't staying in all the time, but rather staying in more of the time than not. Over time it becomes more the norm and even in the most difficult times we do better than we used to. The alignment period is intended for you, as the coach, to do the heavy cleaning with your client, to build the relationship, and set the rules, boundaries, and expectations for the relationship.

Planning

After you've done your heavy cleaning and cleared away old limiting patterns and installed new ones, next is the planning phase of the process. Most coaching systems start here. I suggest you postpone this step for forty days because asking a client to make big life decisions before they are in alignment, feeling good more of the time, and without their new programs at work is a harder way. It takes more work and is less effective. Now that they are in the flow more of the time and feeling good, we can ask the most intelligent part of them what they really want, their heart.

The heart is the most intelligent part of the body. It is tuned to connect directly with the soul. The heart's strong desire is the soul's way of communicating with the rest of you on what path to take for the soul to grow. The purpose of the experience of being on the planet is to be creative and to expand through that creativity. Your soul knows the best way to do that and it will tell you through the heart's desires.

Big Dreams

We use a target and goal planning worksheet to stimulate the process of exposing the heart's desires. We begin by defining what a client's big dreams are. These are the things that they would do if they had unlimited resources. Many times people are so rigid and limited in what they believe is possible that they can't even begin to answer this question. Sometimes we have to prod them. How do we do that? By asking questions. Be mindful not to lead your clients through most of this work. It is more resourceful for them to come up with their own answers rather than agreeing to yours. It also takes creativity to answer for one's self and digging it up will get them thinking differently and exercising parts of their brain they may have not used in a while.

What did you always dream of doing as a kid?

If you won a hundred million dollars in the lottery, what would you do?

If you weren't obligated to the things you think hold you back what would you do?

Let them flow in their creativity and flood the page with stuff. It is important to let them catch their momentum and get into the flow. The reason we start here is because we want to calibrate their inspiration, because in a moment when we go into the specific goal portion, it will seem easy after we stretched them out by thinking beyond what they used to believe was possible.

When discussing their big dreams you will want them to focus on specifics by asking them questions about different areas of their life. Ask them about how they want to feel emotionally, in their intimate relationship, their relationships in general, family life, in their career or business, financially, socially, physically, mentally, spiritually, and including what kind of stuff do they want?

Goals

Next we want to bring them back to Earth and begin focusing on life as it is, and where they want to take it over the next year to five years. Here are some questions to bring that to the surface.

What do you need to do in the area of Personal Development to move closer to your dreams, and that you can achieve in the short to medium term?

What education or other specialized knowledge will you pursue to move closer to the life you want and that you can achieve in the short to medium term?

What do you want from yourself Physically to change in the short to medium term?

What are some things you could do to enrich your life Spiritually that will bring you closer to the life you want?

What do you want to earn Financially?

What other goals do you have to move towards the life you want?

Next extract the goals from the responses and list them.

Find out where the client currently is in relationship to each goal. Are they at the beginning of taking action towards it, or are they already in pursuit towards it? If they have, where are they in that process? Follow this up by taking note of what the next step is that must be made to achieve the goal, and create a deadline to complete this step as well as any other steps that they are aware of in the process. Be sure to track this information as you will want to check in with them and be their accountability partner in tracking the steps and meeting or changing deadlines.

The purpose of the deadline is not always about actually meeting it. Instead it is used more to keep things on track, and to provide a timeline for checking in. Deadlines will inevitably change based on circumstances both within and outside of the client's control. Use them as guideposts, not as rigid requirements. It is important to work within the plan you are creating together and be flexible enough to allow the plan to manifest according to things that are outside of the client's control all the while assisting them to stay on track. Life is a work in progress and so will be your coaching relationship.

The actual purpose of this part of the process is less about how these things will happen, though it is helpful in that area. It is more of a tool to get them to focus more clearly on their intent and to install the emotional resources required to get there. It also plays to the linear, logical, and analytical aspects of their mind which is helpful. Getting the whole brain on board is almost always a good thing. Be careful not to get too attached and rigid in your expectations. It almost always works out better than we plan and may take longer than we expect. That's the beauty of the unconscious and the Universe: they know how long to incubate, germinate, and exactly when to birth things into existence, better than we could logically plan it out.

During the planning time is when you will want to pay close attention to the client's emotional needs. If they are lacking positive emotional resources to implement their plan, it is your job to help them to create them: emotions like determination, motivation, certainty, eagerness, enthusiasm, anticipation, and a whole lot of pleasure. If they don't enjoy it, they aren't going to do it, and if they don't fully understand the consequences of not getting the job done, they are also likely to put it off. You will want to saturate them with strong resourceful emotions around what they want to do and life will improve for them.

Next we are going to create unconscious emotional investment. This is the part of the process that is the missing link between why you achieve some goals and don't make others. It's time to get the unconscious on board and have them going full throttle into this plan, time to think about the big "Why" we talked about earlier in this book. When you define the why you create strong motivation.

Also mentioned earlier all human behavior is motivated towards the good stuff and away from the bad stuff, and when you identify what that is, you create a powerful motivation and increase the likelihood of accomplishing those things you desire.

Have your client take each goal and describe in detail the good things that will happen when they take action and succeed at what they want. Have the client define in clear detail what they expect will happen for them and how they will feel when this is accomplished. Have them imagine what it will be like and describe the outcome to you. Next, ask them to define in detail the consequences that will be avoided by reaching the goal, just as they did before. Be sure to go into detail and dig deep. The bigger the why, the more the likelihood of success. Think of this as the carrot and the stick. Two strong forces, one pushing from behind and the other pulling from ahead, powerfully motivating them towards the outcome they want.

Implementation & Measurement

Now that you have defined the big dreams and goals, and listed the steps to achieve those goals, created a timeline, and installed high levels of motivation, it is time to take action. The reason why this process works so effectively is because rather than jumping into planning and action from where they are when you meet them, you take the necessary time to get the client primed and ready, so that they know more clearly than ever what they want and need.

When you create the plan, both you and the client are to document the goals and timelines. Check in on a weekly basis about where they are in relationship to the plan and if the deadlines are being met or need to be readjusted. The plan <u>will change</u> as the process unfolds. It is important that you and the client track these changes and keep the target and goal planning worksheet as a living, breathing, changing document between you two. This creates accountability and follow-through on the client's part, and thus they are significantly more likely to accomplish what they set out to do.

Think about the alignment period of this process as the pre-game ritual we discussed at the end of the last chapter. This is the big pre-game ritual for your client before they do the real game of creating their life on purpose. They are doing their rituals every day to shake up their own neurology, getting into a peak state, and ironing out old limitations. All the while you are getting in there once a week and influencing deep unconscious change in their belief systems, shifting how they identify, changing their value structure, and giving them new skills. Ultimately you are teaching them how to think smarter and to feel better.

The outcome from this alignment period is always a better understanding of who they truly are and what they really want from life. The most powerful shift I've witnessed personally and with my clients over the years is a new understanding of what is possible. Things become less confusing and complicated and much more simple: step by step, everything becomes more approachable. They will make sacrifices, and the only sacrifices they will have to make are things of a lower nature for a higher nature, letting go of the old things that used to hold them back and embracing their new realm of possibility as a reality.

This mindset creates an openness of opportunity that allows the planning and implementation stages to go much easier and much more smoothly for both you and the client. The truth is your client is already moving through life planning and implementing. What has changed is the consistency of their state and how they think. When they know it is more important that they feel good and be relaxed before making decisions and taking actions it makes life easier.

Most people spend much of their life cleaning up the mess from bad decisions and spend much of their life in disappointment. The reason is because they miss the vital step of getting themselves into an aligned state before deciding to take action. Think back over your own life experience. How many good decisions that resulted in good action with good results were made when you were afraid, angry, depressed, drunk, stoned, tired, hungry, or lonely? Of those good results, if any, be honest, and ask if they were in spite of your un-resourceful state?

I would estimate that most of those decisions made in an un-resourceful state did not produce good results. They may have turned themselves around eventually. The best part about the past is that it is over. Today is a new day, and knowing this, things will never be the same. Sure you'll screw things up, make mistakes, and bad things are going to happen. What has changed is you and how you show up in these moments and what you do in response.

When you plan for the future and take action from a place of feeling good, life goes better. These good feelings don't know where to start and stop. They leak into all areas of your life. They transform your relationships, your home, your work, everything you do. This is why developing and expanding your consciousness is your top priority, job #1, and takes precedence over everything else. It is more important than your work, your significant other, your kids, and what you think you should do, because it is the foundation upon which everything else is built.

Once you truly understand this and use the tools, processes, strategies, and techniques to guide and develop yourself and your clients into this expansion all matter of the Universe comes to meet you. When you combine the powerful force of the human heart, with the strong desire to merge with your true nature, along with the loving and benevolent Universe, this is when seemingly miracles begin to show up for you and your clients more of the time.

This is what we do with our clients rather than for them. They do the work, we walk along their side for this moment in time, and we work through our own powerful connection to be there in ways they cannot be there for themselves, yet. We teach them how to mold and shape themselves into higher functioning beings, and eventually they go on to do it for themselves and maybe even to assist others.

There is a Christian proverb that states "Give a man a fish, feed him for a day. Teach a man to fish, feed him for a lifetime." I love the intention and the message of this proverb. The truth is as a coach, as any teacher, we do both. We feed and we teach. We give nourishment and we teach how to nourish the mind, the body, and the soul. It is in this moment that you truly understand the timeline within which we work is temporary.

This is all temporary, fleeting, and an illusion, constructed as a place of learning and development of something much bigger than this world. Your intention with every client is to work yourself out of a job as quickly as possible with each person you meet, and to know that this, as well as all things of this world, will come to an end which means there will be a new beginning too.

PRACTICE MANAGEMENT

"Begin with the end in mind."

— Stephen Covey

You will want to stay organized from the very beginning because when you start to get really busy, it is going to be a lot easier to already have the systems in place to support you rather than trying to clean it up in the aftermath. I know this from experience. I didn't plan on being as successful as I am, and now have paid the price for not having the foresight to prepare in advance. It is like trying to change a tire while driving down the road.

First things first: contacts, contacts, contacts. You will inevitably meet a lot of people over the course of building your successful coaching business. Get in the habit now of organizing and tracking your contact with them. Set a day and time to enter their full information into your database and email list, or hire an assistant to manage this for you. Make notes on the prospects in your database. Include spouse's names, children's names, other key people like their assistant's name, front line managers, anyone who is vital to them in maintaining their life, their work or business, and their survival. Also create relationships, if appropriate, with these people that support your client, as they will only make your life easier.

Track and note important dates and set up reminders on your calendar about these dates. This will include their birthday, anniversary, and other important milestones for them. You will want to send them a handwritten card before these dates. This is an added touch of professionalism. You'll notice that I said handwritten card, not an email, Facebook post, or text message. It may seem old fashioned, but it demonstrates that you care and that you are invested in a relationship over the years ahead. I also suggest sending them a gift when they sign with you, perhaps a quality journal. I like to give a nice leather bound journal or one from Papaya (www.papayaart.com) depending on the type of client I'm working with and always without lines. Journals without lines can drive people crazy and force them to be more creative. I'm always on the hunt for ways to push my clients out of their comfort zone.

When documenting your client's important dates in their file and in your note also include the date their contract comes up for renewal. I have a running list of active clients in my notes program that is shared through my iCloud on my phone and computer. It has the client's names and the date that their contract expires. Also put these dates into your calendar. Put a reminder in your calendar thirty days before the expiration to remind you to discuss it with them in upcoming sessions. This will enable them to consider extending their professional relationship with you and prepare for renewal, or to wrap up over the next thirty days.

When you have a fully booked practice, tracking the multitudes of information can be challenging. What I suggest is that you start organizing these things ahead of time while your practice is small so you can avoid being overwhelmed when things get really busy. I also recommend that you start your coaching agreements with your clients on the first or fifteenth of the month. Even if this means they get a small number of additional weekly sessions free, because it makes tracking your renewals easier. Do not ever short a client when you take on this strategy. Always under promise, and over deliver. It's a law of nature, give more than you receive and give more than you take away. I suggest you intend on giving your clients ten times more in intrinsic value than what you receive in financial value from them.

Confidential Client Questionnaire

At the end of introductory session, during which you explain the daily activities for success, you will send them home with the confidential client questionnaire. This questionnaire is to be filled out and returned to you forty-eight hours before your next meeting with them. This questionnaire will give you useful information to assist them in their process and give you a very powerful platform for discussion. It will allow you to unearth the deeper beliefs and thought structures they use to succeed, or those that are limiting them from creating what they want.

During the second session with your new client, you will discuss the confidential client questionnaire and have them expand on their responses. At the end of this session you will then introduce the pre-call form.

Pre-Call Form

One way that I track my clients and where they are in the process is through a pre-call form. This form is completed before each and every session and emailed to me in PDF form forty-eight hours before our session. PDF guarantees that no matter what the device I'm using to access it there is a high likelihood that I'll be able to view it. This form updates me of where the client is in the coaching process and also allows me to prepare for the call. It also begins installing important reflections and resources for the client that have come as a result of the homework they did by the questions that the form asks. Here is a copy of the form we use:

Complete Answers individually for **each** of the tasks that were assigned during your last session or as a result of communication since then:

The exercise(s) I was to complete was:

1. I found this exercise: easy, moderate, difficult, or extremely difficult and explain why:

2. I was successful/unsuccessful at this exercise because:

3. I learned (became aware of) the following during the execution of this exercise:

4. I feel this exercise will positively affect my life/work/business in the future in the following way:

5. My additional reflections are:

6. Questions for my coach:

7. Brief Update regarding your life/work/business not included in the above responses:

By asking the client for this information in this way we create another layer of learning because they are given the opportunity to take the time to focus, consider, and plan at a deeper level the experience they are creating through the process they have completed. It also allows the coach to use this response along with any questions they have and updates about their life/work/business to be more prepared for the session.

In the beginning the client can be a bit overwhelmed with the number of tasks they are completing and changes that they are implementing. Because they are doing the daily activities for success and they are completing any homework assignments, it is reasonable that for the first couple of sessions they might forget to complete the pre-call form. It is important that you send them an email and remind them to send it to you and address it in the next session. You are not a schoolmarm, though it is important to demonstrate in the beginning and throughout the coaching process that they are accountable to you and that you will provide them with a gentle reminder.

Accountability is much of what we do on the surface throughout the professional relationship with our clients. It is important that we are able to track and maintain what is going on with our client, and more importantly, train them to do it for themselves. Remember our job is to coach ourselves out of a job. While we are tracking the accountability of our clients we want to make that responsibility theirs.

I suggest keeping a file electronically or a dedicated notebook for each of your clients. During each session keep notes of things you discussed, processes you did, and the assignments they were to complete. Be sure to organize it and split the different subjects into different parts of the entry, because otherwise you will have to sift it out when you go to review it and this wastes time. If you don't see an item from your notes mentioned in the pre-call form, bring it up during the session and ask them the questions from the pre-call form. Do not mix notes from different clients in one notebook or file. Dedicate a notebook or file to each client. It will save you a lot of trouble and searching later. Organization is key to tracking data and staying focused.

After the alignment period of the coaching relationship, you will want to have the client complete a planning process as we discussed earlier. In their file and/or dedicated notebook track where they are in the process each week, the next steps to the process, new or changed goals, and the new or changed deadlines to complete these tasks. Every session update these changes. Review these notes before each session along with the pre-call form. This will motivate the process forward, engage your client to be accountable to you and themselves, and teach them how to maintain progress using a similar system.

Renewal

Thirty days before your contract with your client expires, your calendar will notify you because you set this reminder after they signed your coaching agreement and you received your initial payment. This is when you want to do the measurement aspect of this process. Ask your client a series of questions to find out what they have achieved, how they have changed, and what they have valued about the experience thus far. Be sure to get a lot of responses to these questions and that they explain themselves fully. Have them give as accurate and exact of measurements as well as they can. If further research is required to get these measurements then make that part of their homework assignment and take note in their file/notebook.

Pull out the original Target and Goal Planning document they completed when you first started the planning component of the coaching process. Take notes of how things have progressed since the inception of this document. If there are missing measurements check in with the client and ask them where they are in relation to their goals. Also find out what has happened as a "positive side effect" of their coaching experience that isn't on the list.

More often than not a client will achieve, create, manifest, and have positive experiences and results that they didn't plan to have happen. These seem almost miraculous in some cases. These have included finding true love, getting a dream job, being inspired to move across the country or the world to start a new amazing life, and saving a marriage that at the time seemed destined to fail. These unplanned positive side effects are the direct result of the client getting out of their own way and allowing it as a result of the work we do. Be sure to elicit these important milestones from the client and document them.

Following this measurement check-in, ask them what their thoughts are about where they want the relationship to go next. This question is driving them to define in detail why they believe they should continue working with you, if they do. You're not necessarily always going to want get your client to renew with you. You and your client can evaluate together if that is appropriate. In almost all cases I work with clients for one year, sometimes longer, and sometimes only for six months. I have even worked with clients for only a handful of months and because of the work that was done and the results they got they were more than satisfied and paid the full fee.

The coaching process is organic and unfolds in the client's energy and learning process. We aren't creating clients for years, rather we are with them until they have learned to do much of what we do for them for themselves and hopefully others too. When you work with precision to remove thinking that gets in their way and to optimize them and their well-being, all matter of solutions are possible and come into fruition.

Asking for Referrals

Referrals are a critical for building the success of any business. Word of mouth is how things sell. You can spend a fortune on promotion and get a room full of people to listen to you. What will get their friends and family to buy from you is their opinion of you and how they talk about you. People want to help people they like be successful. This is one of the reasons it is so very important to build a relationship with your clients. They become your friend, your cheerleader, and a member of your marketing team. One quality referral is worth a hundred cold calls.

You are 90% more likely to get a referral if you ask for it. Even clients who talk about you in high praise to the people they know will do so and not send them as an actual referral. It isn't because they don't want to, it is because they need to be reminded, in some cases prodded, and told how to. I suggest that you ask for referrals immediately after you close your new client. It sets the stage, breaks the ice around the topic, and prepares them for the next time you ask.

I use the following sentence when introducing the concept of referrals "Also, I'm wondering who you know that is like you, that you like, and may also benefit from working with me, enjoy a complimentary session, and would make a good referral. Referrals are how I build my business and I appreciate your help doing that. Who do you know that [fill in with the description of your target candidate]?" Then do one of the most powerful sales techniques out there, Shut Up.

Especially after you did the delicate work of closing the sale, if the client doesn't have anyone in mind, since they are on the spot, I suggest dropping it. Pushing now seems unnecessary and could cause discomfort for them. It is important to do it though, plant the seed and tell them to consider it between now and their first session; and when someone does comes to mind, they will be more apt to take note and then you can discuss an introduction.

Another great time to ask for referrals is when the client experiences a big win that is directly connected to the work you two are doing together. In this high of their success, of course, they want others to know about you. Who is the question? Ask them and do so eloquently. This is also a good time to ask for a written or video testimonial. More evidence of how awesome you are for others who are considering your services.

Time Management

"Early is on time, on time is late" your new time mantra.

This mantra was taught to me by one of my first mentors when I joined the financial services industry. If I had a client meeting at 8AM, it was my job to show up at 7:30AM. If we were going to have a staff meeting at 11AM everyone was expected to be in the conference room at 10:55. The meeting started at 11 and coming into the room at that time was unacceptable, inconsiderate, and poor planning.

It becomes a metaphor for life. Are you going to show up just a few minutes late for life and if so how much time will that add up to over a lifetime? As coaches it is very risky business to market ourselves as someone that can come into a person's life and radically help them achieve something if we ourselves lack self-discipline and accountability.

Now is the time to take your own personal level of follow through and organization to a new level of professionalism and strength. It's time to take your commitments over the edge. It's time to show up early, follow through, and to be known as a top level professional that walks their talk. Remember to "under-promise and over-deliver" in all areas of your life. This minimizes disappointment and over-satisfies your relationships. It also creates a nice buffer and gives you a lot of leeway when you do inevitably screw up.

Today the excuse maker dies, and in the very rare case that you fall short on the commitment, you make amends for it immediately, minimize the reasoning or explanation which when over-indulged can be confused for excuses, and you make it right. If your violation is a pattern, your amends isn't an amends until you change. As a result of your new level of commitment and general consistency forgiveness won't even take a second thought by the people in your life. Time is the most finite resource on the planet for all of us. You were born and will die. It's up to you how you use each moment in between and that adds up to hours, days, months, and years. This is a direct reflection of how you value life and the experience that comes with it.

I have heard about the teachings that you really want to "be here now." That is important. The only problem is that it is an awfully ambitious statement. It is preached like it is the superior concept of time. But, it is only one perspective of time and experience. If you are always in the now, you can't heal the past or go into the future to plan. Personal power is being able to be in the now when you choose. Most people don't have control of where their mind is focused most of the time. They get pushed back into the past and pulled into the future by the whims of their monkey mind and the distractions of the world around them.

There is power in being in the now and also consciously moving above, below, inside, outside, and through time in your mind with purpose. Our neurology constructs time through the representational systems. In simple terms *time simply isn't real.* It is imagined and created. How you construct your reality is based significantly on how you think of time. It directly influences how and when you create your experience.

The perception of time influences balance and leads to fulfillment. For our discussion let's imagine there are three types of time. We will color code them as red time, blue time, and green time.

Red Time

Red time is defined as personal time. Personal time is the most important time on your schedule. This does not mean that it consumes your calendar, rather, that is takes priority over all other events. Red means stop and take care of yourself and your life.

As busy business people and successful achievers, we often neglect our personal time because we think that productivity and achieving is more important. Wrong. We often believe this because it has tangible rewards attached to it and gives us significance.

Alignment is the direct result of things you do with your personal time and without it your life falls victim to the ego and the illusion of the physical world. Personal time is the variable that balances being a supercharged spiritual being and the physical world. It is the reservoir, the gas station, the pit stop to tune up to live the purpose we are here to serve.

The time you spend with your loved ones, working out and taking care of your body, meditating, playing, being creative and resting is the secret to a fulfilling life. When you get out to the end of your timeline and saying goodbye to your physical life on earth, you aren't going to count up the assets, acquisitions, achievements, and how productive you were. It is more likely you are going to value the small important things, the magic moments, the ordinary rituals of life and the love that you shared with the most important people to you.

Money and achievements have never satisfied anyone on the deepest level. In order to sustain fulfillment and to add to it, we must take the time to create the small substantial moments. We do this by playing with our family and our loved ones and taking care of ourselves. Our top priority and number one job, in both our personal and business life, is to feel good more of the time. In order to do this we must make sure our schedule has a healthy balance of personal time to take care of ourselves, and connect with the people important to us. Soon enough they will be gone or we will leave them, that is inevitable and the nature of our physical existence. You can't get it back, so practice taking advantage of it all now and in the future.

Blue Time

Blue time is preparation time. This is the time you spend working ON your business. Many coaches in the beginning distract themselves with blue time activities like writing emails, creating business cards and flyers, planning webinars and products, and shuffling paperwork. These activities are important and can lead to valuable results over the medium to long term or are required to maintain your business. Make sure that you manage the amount of time you spend doing these things and, in most cases, limit it to no more than a third of your work time. In the beginning, creating short term revenue is more important than pursuing activities that might lead to payoffs over time. Many new coaches get distracted in blue time activities when they need to be out making contacts, performing complimentary sessions, and serving their clients and getting referrals. Avoid this pitfall, and work in your business and on your business each a third of the time.

Green Time

Next, are green time activities. Think green, like money; this is when the revenue comes into your business, also known as income. These include activities like making contacts and prospecting, complimentary sessions, and serving your clients. How can you tell the difference between a blue time activity and a green time activity? The answer is simple. We use a test in the form of a question. "Will this activity *potentially* result in generating revenue within fourteen days?"

If the answer is yes, you have a green time activity. If no, then you have a blue time activity. If it's a blue time activity, then the result will be medium to long term. Activities like calling prospects to schedule complimentary sessions, networking and social events, following up on prospective clients are all examples of green time activities.

Creating a seminar, writing an article for publication, publishing a brochure, blogging, creating a book, writing stories for speaking are all examples of blue time activities. These activities are considered blue time activities because they have the possibility of leading to revenue eventually but not within fourteen days. Do these things and build your business and manage how much of your time you focus on doing them. Be careful to properly manage your time and be realistic about what activities lead to short-term revenue and what may pay off eventually.

It's important to differentiate between blue time and green time activities because in the beginning of building your coaching business it's important to focus on green time activities to create revenue and get cash flowing. Think of the green time activities as the lifeblood of your business; without green time it dies. Blue time activities manage your business and plan for how that life blood will come in, eventually, in the future. Both are important, and your job is to balance them, along with your personal time.

Hiding behind your desk and playing on your computer and rationalizing that it will lead to revenue in the future is dangerous. In sales it happens far too often. It's one of the main reasons I consider one of the qualifications required to be a coach is to already be successful. Successful people focus their effort and energy into what is vital to succeed and outsource or delegate the other activities to their team or other companies. Most importantly they associate a high level of pleasure to vital business building activities and enjoy it. Learn to enjoy the activities that build your business and your success will follow as a result.

As a coach you are the ultimate sales person. Your job is to get out and create relationships and demonstrate how you impact people and organizations. You are the product and the service. No brochure, no website, no business card will ever accurately represent that. Your clients need to see you, hear you, and feel what you bring to the world.

In the first three years of business I never carried a card and didn't have a web site and I earned well over six figures a year. The blue time tools mentioned above have value, especially as your business matures, and it is a false premise that they will make you a thought leader in the industry or earn you a small fortune without you building first from the ground up. Your presence and your relationships will generate your wealth, and over time, as a result, these tools will amplify the leader who you truly are.

The key to all of this is understanding the critical value of maintaining a balance of the three types of time. Do yourself the service and schedule them on your calendar. Block out your personal time activities. I primarily work with one-on-one clients on Tuesday, Wednesday, and Thursday. This gives me the weekends to do seminars, events, and for personal time. I also like to utilize Mondays and Fridays to do blue time activities. I also have an assistant who handles many of these blue time activities for me. It takes green time to pay someone to do blue time and create more freedom for red time.

Schedule recurring events, individual events, and client times on your calendar. Also block out times when you do not want to see clients. This will help you to stay on track. Be sure to evaluate your calendar and take careful consideration if there is too much or too little time being spent in red, blue, or green time. In an ideal world your waking time will be balanced equally between all three.

I schedule my clients for ninety minute sessions. There are a variety of reasons I do this. One is because I run about an hour session and use the last 20-30 minutes for deep trance work and to wrap up the call. It also gives me a few minutes between calls if need be. I know coaches that do thirty to forty minute calls and that may very well work for them, but I don't find it is enough time to do the work on the level that I personally perform.

Become a master at communicating because the majority of our work is communication including emails, phone calls, meetings, seminars, trainings, and client sessions. If we are inconsistent about performing these activities, we lose credibility and don't provide the real or perceived value we promise. My clients receive a weekly scheduled session, unlimited on the fly sessions, and unlimited email communication.

In the coaching agreement I use, I commit to respond to our client emails and requests for a session within twenty-four hours of receiving their email. This is a good commitment to have in place for all of your relationships, not only your clients. It will keep you organized and on top of the ever growing pile of communications. This pile doesn't get smaller the more successful you are, so create good habits about managing it now. This will serve you profoundly when the tsunami hits.

Create a note or working document called "Important Dates." List the events you are committed and obligated to, and the duration of the dates you will be there in sequence. Be sure to account for travel time if there is any. When writing out the dates include the actual days of the week for example: Monday, September 22 to Friday, October 3rd. This way you can quickly reference this single document when scheduling and planning future commitments rather than having to go through your calendar and digging up the information. Make sure both professional and personal items make it to this list. If you have a personal assistant, make sure they know and are given access so that they may further help you. These are simple tips and will keep you much more organized as your practice blossoms.

When scheduling clients I recommend that you have their time slot reoccurring at the same time and same day each week. Be sure to confirm with them at the end of each session this will work for the following week. It is important that you both notify each other if there is a schedule change within twenty-four hours before the session and reschedule the session immediately and within the next couple days. This will help avoid having the rescheduled session and their next session squeezed to closely together.

More than anything be sure to use systems that are easy to organize yourself. These systems I'm suggesting may not best suit you. Use your creativity to modify and create systems that do work best for you and can be easily duplicated when you bring in assistance. Simplicity is key. Be sure to start building lists and keep them updated. Most sales people miss opportunities because they aren't organized and lack a good plan. It seems odd to think that you would forget to follow up on a prospective client but it happens far too often. Teach your clients to be self-accountable and demonstrate what you expect and then reinforce the boundaries when you need to for them and yourself.

Years ago I was working with a client who just would not follow through with her responsibilities. She struggled doing the daily activities for success; she haphazardly did her assignments, and she never sent her pre-call forms. In the beginning I was patient and gentle with her until I realized that this approach just wasn't working.

It made me think of, Kerri Strug winning the Olympic gold medal in 1996, with a broken ankle. If you watch the video of this monumental event just before she wins, her coach, Béla Károlyi, literally yells in her face "You can do this! You will do this! You can do this! You will do this! You can do this! You will do this!" over and over again. You can see him spraying her with a mist of spit as he yells at her. She stands there deep in trance and spinning powerful emotional resources of certainty, determination, and strong motivation. A moment later she has an impeccable performance and as you know wins the gold in spite of her very serious injury.

For some reason this client and I were doing our session in a restaurant. I highly advise against doing complimentary and regular sessions with clients in a public setting as I have said before. They are distracting and can create unwanted attention. I confronted her and was flexible enough to be strong, direct, and intervene in a very powerful way. My coaches and I call this "Panthering." We become the panther and walk softly, wait quietly, and when the moment arrives we pounce on our prey and eat them alive. Some situations require that you do this for yourself and others. It isn't my first go-to tool, but it was very appropriate for this situation.

I held steadfast in my determination to get her to change and to take on life in an entirely new way. She needed conviction, determination, and motivation and I gave it to her. She started crying and sobbing uncontrollably. I don't think anyone had ever held her accountable or was more flexible than her to make it stick.

She looked me in the eyes and asked between wailings "Why are you doing this to me? Making me cry in front of all these people?"

"Because you changing is more important than what a handful of people you don't even know or will ever see again think of you! Wouldn't you agree?"

Her unconscious mind understood me because it was close enough to hear me in this altered state. She started showing up early, doing her homework, sending the pre-call forms, and had an entirely new attitude. She started her own business and got two big accounts that earned her over a hundred thousand dollars in a few months. Not long after, she met the love of her life who she married three years later.

I'm not saying embarrassing her publicly or making her cry is what changed her. It was being flexible enough to hold her accountable and to not waiver in my expectation, and making sure I stayed determined with the conviction that was required to make the change whatever it took. You are the example and your job is to demonstrate that in all you do personally and in your profession. Create boundaries, stick to them, with both yourself and your client, and thrive as a result.

PART 3: BUILDING MOMENTUM

Successful investors enjoy some of their profits and reinvest most of them into intelligent opportunities to multiply their wealth over time. This is called compounding. You want to think of where you focus your time and energy also, as an investment that compounds over time. Even if you are at the beginning of building your coaching business, it is important to create a powerful momentum that will lead you to the success of the practice you desire now.

The following final chapters will teach you how to build this momentum going forward. They are critical to showcase your place in the world and to give you credibility as a resource to create a powerful impact.

As you experience greater success, there are natural side-effects that come from this: wealth, power, influence, and relationships with people who also have these resources. It is important to understand how this works, and to plan for this kind of success now, so you can prepare for it. There is great responsibility that comes with the work you are going into. It is good to know what is coming and how to mold it into place because you can either ride the wave or be swept away with it. The difference is how you plan and execute the natural momentum that will come.

SPEAK

"A good speech should be like a woman's skirt; long enough to cover the subject and short enough to create interest."

— Winston Churchill

If you are going to be in this business for any time at all and be successful you will, if only out of necessity, be required to speak to a group of people. Speaking is one of the most valuable tools we have in our business, whether that is one on one or to a group. We talk to people. The longer you are in this business the more people you will speak to, it is inevitable. If you want to earn $250,000 or more a year, then you will speak to groups as a keynote speaker and in seminars that you will teach. It is an inevitable side-effect of being a successful coach.

Public speaking is the number one phobia on the planet, usually caused by insensitive and sometimes mean spirited teachers that embarrassed and ridiculed the person through shame as a child in front of their peers. This trauma creates a long lasting scar on the psyche and anchors deep anxiety and panic to speaking.

In seminars with Dr. Bandler, in London, one of the segments is about the "fast phobia cure." We group participants according to their phobia. We have the creature station with snakes and spiders, the claustrophobics, those with a fear of needles, heights and flying fears, and public speaking. Usually about eighty percent of the people end up in the public speaking phobia group. Someone with a fear of speaking may be great one on one, and when put in front of a group, even a small one, will shut down and freak out. It doesn't make any rational sense, but it happens a lot.

If you have a speaking phobia or strong fear, you can easily remove it by doing the fast phobia cure created by Dr. Richard Bandler. It is as the name implies, fast, easy, and effective.

Here's how to do it:

Disassociate and watch yourself from the outside. Create a movie of what happens when you get scared about speaking to a group of people. Rather than being in the movie and having the experience watch yourself from the outside. Notice what happens in the movie, all the while staying in the observer position.

Watch it all the way to the end of the movie then freeze it at the end, the very last slide of the movie.

Change the movie to black and white; float into the movie and associate with it, meaning become the person *IN* the movie.

Then run the movie backwards from the end all the way back to the beginning as quickly as possible all the while making funny sounds or carnival music. The people in the movie walk backwards, talk backwards, everything goes backwards all the way back to the beginning of the movie.

When you get back to the beginning, turn the movie bright white. Fill your entire mind with this bright white.

When you do this the old neurological pathways flatten out and it just isn't possible on a neurological level to get that old feeling of fear back, even if you try. It's the same as if you were to tear up an old highway. You just can't go that way anymore so your mind has to go a different way, perhaps curious, eager, and desirous.

Repeat this process a few times. As with most internal processing neurological techniques, it may be difficult to do this on yourself, though it is possible. It is better to have a licensed practitioner of NLP® do this for you, or become one yourself. This is just one of numerous examples of extremely effective and beneficial technologies provided by NLP®, which is why we train and certify all of our coaches as licensed NLP® practitioners.

It seems simple, and it is. What is important is that it works. Sometimes the simplest way in life is the most effective, and if you're anything like me you like to do things the fastest and most efficient way you can. That is why I have written this book. I used these strategies to make a pile of money and then invested that money into learning the most powerful technologies on the planet and worked with the people who knew the most about them. Most of what is in this book is what I did to get here. What I learned afterward is another book entirely in itself, or perhaps a few. There is so much to this magical world we live in.

Once the fear of speaking is gone and replaced with good feelings like pleasure, eagerness, anticipation, and fun it is time to get the skills of a professional speaker. You may have notice I didn't say public speaker. Anyone can have the confidence to speak publicly, but there are much fewer who can speak professionally. Being a professional implies that you know how to do something very well and that you ought to be paid very well to do it. I want to make clear the difference because much of what I'm going to share with you is not what toastmasters or the national speakers association teaches. I'm going to teach you how to do what they don't do, which will make you even better.

The word alignment is where we begin. Canceling out a lifelong phobia or big fear of speaking in front of people is getting more into alignment with what you desire. The next step is getting into the right state. There is a state that is optimal for doing most things. Some people think that in order to be great you have to be over the top, loud, and bigger than life. Yes, sometimes that is how a great speaker will appear, but I can tell you that is not the state they are in, if they are really good. It also may not be the most effective way to influence your audience.

The state you're aiming for is relaxed and calm, where time slows down. It is as if you are driving down the highway at a hundred miles per hour and you are looking out over the horizon; in your peripheral vision telephone poles are whipping by along with the yellow dotted lines on the highway and you pull off the exit. There is a school zone and you slow down to fifteen... miles... per... hour. It is as if time is moving a glacial pace. Things seem to be going in extremely slow motion. This is the state that martial artists go into when they prepare for a fight. They see the strike coming from miles away. They plan their defense and their counter attack in nano-seconds and then when the time comes they take action without thought, unconsciously.

This state is so critical because it is natural for your body to release adrenaline into the system when you step in front of a crowd. This is a very good thing. The question is what feeling are you going to associate with it? Feeling good and having a spike of adrenaline is a good combination for speaking to others. There is a profound difference in the energy of a group than talking to a couple of people. This spike is going to give you the energy to excel.

When you are speaking you are doing many things at once. In order to do them well you need more time. There is only the time you are allotted and you want to keep your audience's attention, therefore the only way for you to get more time without appearing strange is to slow down your perception of it. You connect with your audience by observing them. By being in front of them you have the advantage because you can see them and gage their responses.

One way people like to freak themselves out is by imagining the audience before they see them. They make scary pictures that are bigger than life, imagining the worst and then wonder why they are so freaked out. The truth is that your audience, if only for a moment, is very open to you, interested, and inviting. If they are not, then you may want to reconsider what kind of speaking gigs you are saying yes to. So, plan ahead, and make a better plan by making different pictures that feel good. They are closer to reality than the torture chamber you might have been hanging out in. See their interested faces and hear their accepting responses.

In most cases you'll have someone that will introduce you. Write your own introduction. Keep it light and precise, and it is okay to brag a little bit, but do not go overboard. It is better to have someone else build you up rather than directly doing it yourself. Also write the introduction specifically tailored to the event so that it will create interest from the participants. Ask the person introducing you to add a couple lines about what they think about you or how they know you only if they are familiar with you. Keep this introduction short and sweet. You want to preserve time for your presentation. This is especially important if you are doing a keynote address which is usually only somewhere between thirty to forty five minutes. This may seem like a long time, but in reality it is a blip of time and every minute counts. Be sure to make eye contact with the person introducing you and shake their hand or give them a light hug, and to thank them for introducing you.

When you step out on stage you want to be in that aligned state feeling really good with your perception of time dramatically slowed down. Be like Mohammed Ali, float like a butterfly and sting like a bee. Almost all presenters speak too quickly as a side effect of their excitement and the adrenaline factor. Mastery comes with the ability to slow down and speed up on purpose, with intent and along with what you are saying. This means that the speed at which you speak is under your control and appropriate for what you are talking about.

The rate at which you speak will influence the breathing of your audience. People automatically fall into sync with the speaker and will breath at the pace and the rhythm of the speaker. This is powerful when you use it to your advantage. When you speak too fast or too slow, you affect your audience and create a connection or a disconnection. This is why being able to observe your audience is so important.

Keep your gestures and movement around the stage to a minimum. Be precise about your movements and only use them for effect and to add to your talk. Presenters that move around a lot and use a lot of unnecessary gestures actually distract from their message. Treat your space as an empty canvas, and when you move know that you are painting on that canvas and affecting the minds of those watching you. This is not to say hold completely still, rather move with purpose and intent with the words, ideas, concepts, and emotions that you are presenting. The most powerful speaker can be completely still and captivate their audience, if they choose to because they have the control and the discipline.

Always be taking note of your audience and notice their responses and interest level. Your number one competitor is not the speaker before you or after you. It is the smart phone or tablet in the audience member's hand. These days, people have such an incredibly short attention span that if you don't suck them in and keep them entertained from the very beginning, they will turn to their mobile device: scrolling through the newsfeed on Facebook, looking at pictures on Instagram, fighting with their spouse over text message, or just to stare at it in a trance. It is sad but true. If you are going to be a professional you have to hook them in fast, and keep them entertained.

It doesn't matter whether you are a keynote speaker or if you have them in a corporate training, you've got to entertain them. Remember Mrs. Steffen from earlier? She was the teacher that noticed I wasn't learning disabled, rather that I needed to be stimulated and to be bribed. She didn't limit me, she engaged me. You need to think about your audience the same way. They aren't learning disabled. They are smart phone addicted and trained for short bursts of high emotional responses layered one after the other.

Think of your talk as a newsfeed on Facebook, only all the garbage is taken out. This is how you want to craft your talk. A series of strong emotional responses strung together by necessary content that allows it to make sense to your audience and that entertains and keeps them engaged. The best way to do this is to tell stories.

These stories will be short entertaining stories that are for the most part about you. You can certainly tell stories about other people, but those that are about you are the most powerful because this will create a connection to you on the part of your audience. A bond, in any relationship, is created by experiences you share with the other person. We often feel a strong bond with celebrities we don't know and have never met because we know so much of their personal story and thus have a strong feeling of connection with them.

Connection is the energy you are going for with your audience. I'm not suggesting that you just ramble and tell stories for the sake of telling stories. Tell good stories that get a high impact of emotional responses from your listeners. You know the stories I'm talking about. You have many of them already. These are the stories that when you tell them, almost every time the person you tell them to has a strong emotional response. Perhaps they cry, feel encouraged, become hopeful, or burst out laughing. The best stories have a variety of these strong emotional responses laced throughout them.

It is important when telling these stories to a group that you do not sound like a public speaker. The fastest way to disconnect from your audience, regardless of how entertaining your story may be, is to be overly formal. The way to connect with an audience and further the connection of that bond is to speak conversationally. At toastmasters they ring a bell when you say an "um." Um is ok. I'm not suggesting that you stutter with "ums" throughout your presentation, but don't get too caught up in the perfection of your talk. Perfectionism separates the human element from the people that are sitting before us and they want to feel like you are a real person. Be authentic; audiences move towards the real authentic you and away from the fake and perfect. Their unconscious knows the difference and when you are trying too hard.

The best speakers on the planet make their audience feel like they are sitting in their living room together. Like they are just hanging out and having a good talk. Start listening to the speakers that you like the best and listen to how they tell stories and talk to their audiences. You'll find the ones you feel more naturally connected to speak like they are having a conversation by the fire or in a bar. Tell some great stories that are personal and get your audience feeling their emotions.

In this business content is everything. For our purposes we only want two types of content. The first type of content gets those high emotional responses we've been talking about. These are the six second Vine videos on your newsfeed that you watch over and over again and have you in stitches. These are the parts of the stories that get tears, laughter, hope, inspiration, regret, pain, and pleasure.

The second kind is the content that allows the story to make sense. If this information wasn't there the story would fall apart and the emotional response you get will be confusion. Now most of us don't come out of the womb knowing which information is which. So this is where planning and testing come into play. It is important that you write out your stories in a conversational style. Write them out the same way you would tell them to your best friend or significant other. Remember you want your audience to feel like they are hanging out with you not being lectured.

Next, begin analyzing the story and highlight what parts of it really get a strong emotional response. We aren't judging pleasurable or painful emotions because a strong emotional response is good regardless of which kind it is. Later you'll layer these stories together and both the resourceful and un-resourceful states will come in handy depending on what you are wanting to do with your audience. After you've pulled out the high emotional responses and the vital information, then evaluate what information is trash and get rid of it. You should ask if it is really vital to keep the story alive or if you can dump it? If it doesn't help the story make sense, or get a strong emotional response, throw it away, right away. Too many times people keep information in a story because they are attached to it. If it doesn't matter that you were wearing your favorite nirvana shirt from your freshmen year strike it out. Less is more, and most people have the problem of telling too much rather than not enough.

After you have sifted, sorted, and taken out the trash now is the time to start testing the stories so you can polish them up. When you are around other people perhaps at dinner or waiting for a meeting to start, tell a story. In most cases they will only be a few minutes long after you get done cleaning them up. As you are telling the story watch and listen for the feedback you get from the people that are listening.

Pay special attention to their emotional responses and take note which part of the stories create the strongest responses. You can tell by their facial expressions, their body movements, their eye movements, and the sounds they make. If they show signs of confusion or boredom, and that isn't intended, take note of where it happens in the story. This is an indicator that something isn't flowing properly and you'll want to edit that part of the message, or add connective information so it makes better sense, or reconsider how you are telling it.

This process works whether you are speaking at a luncheon or giving a week-long training. I know because I've done both. People will put their smart phone down and pay attention when they are given rich, interesting, and engaging content, and to do that well takes planning. It is important that you are constantly developing these stories.

The way you can use them in a training seminar is to choose the stories that best fit the content that you are teaching. People learn best through stories, analogies, and metaphors. They engage deeply with story and you can use it to entertain and demonstrate what you are teaching. Most stories can teach a variety of ideas and concepts without even mentioning what they are teaching which allows your audience to come to their own conclusion making the learning even more powerful or to drive your point in even further. And thus, you can often use the same story in different contexts to introduce and teach extremely varied topics and lessons.

Story Crafting Exercise

Take out your journal and start a running list of interesting personal stories that have happened to you.

Write out the most interesting stories completely and in detail.

Using three different colored highlighters sort out the content based on strong emotional responses, necessary information for the story to make sense, and trash.

Practice telling these stories to other people testing the content and flow. Make adjustments to enhance the experience of the listener.

Memorize these stories and have an accurate estimate of how much time they take to tell.

Remember when telling the story to do so conversationally. Meaning though you have invested significant time polishing it and preparing it, be very careful not to sound perfect or rehearsed. Screw it up on purpose so that it sounds like you're telling it for the first time. Hem, haw, um, and let the story sound natural, imperfect, and real. You'll tell these stories hundreds of times so have fun making them sound natural like a conversation.

Group events can be very profitable, can save you thousands of hours, and demonstrate your abilities to the participants gaining you credibility and more personal clients. For example you can agree to coach a sales person and meet with them an hour a week for six months totaling twenty four hours and earn $4,000. That's not too bad, and a great place to start. Then again you could do a five-day training for ten sales people for $1,500 each, totaling thirty hours of training, and earn $15,000.

The impact is far more significant because you are teaching a lot of content rapidly rather than spreading it over time. This isn't to say you cannot do both; you certainly can, and I would expect you to. What I want to make clear is that if you want to maximize your success and your efficiency it will require you to be able to speak professionally to groups of people. Why stop at ten participants, why not twenty or a hundred. What about a thousand or ten thousand?

This book is dedicated to giving you the tools to create a successful coaching business now. You can take what we have discussed thus far and thrive in private practice. One of the many ways you can build this practice even faster is by talking to groups. Whether that is at luncheons, at the rotary club, or holding your own live weekend retreats, this will give you the opportunity to demonstrate to others, even if for only a few minutes, that you have something special to offer.

You know the energy I'm talking about. You sit there and you listen and watch the presenter and something inside you says there is something special here, an opportunity, something that I need and I want more of it. This will happen to you. People will be in your presence and you will tell your story and things inside them will begin to shift. They will want to talk to you, connect, and learn more about you. How great that you are prepared to work with them and assist them on their path.

When they come to you, they may think they need help with their career, business, or their marriage. We call these perceived needs and they are valid and should be spoken and sold to. What they are really coming to you for is deep personal change, to think differently, feel differently, and do things differently. You begin this conversation and this process when you showcase yourself in front of others. You don't have to be perfect. The person who introduces you will do a good enough job of that. What you need to do is be real, authentic, and tell your story.

People will like you and be attracted to you because of your success, but they will fall in love with you and create a bond with your humanity because of your failures. Tell stories about your mistakes, your failures, and the bad choices you made along the way with fun, playful, and adventurous stories. Speak from your heart and use yourself as the example. Leverage the truth that we are all on this journey, figuring it out one day into the next. You don't sell coaching or tell stories; you give people feelings and feelings my friend are what motivate all human behavior. You master your ability to do that and life on all levels will profoundly change for the better.

MERGE WITH THE BIGGER VISION

"It surprises me how disinterested we are today about things like physics, space, the universe and philosophy of our existence, our purpose, our final destination. It's a crazy world out there. Be curious."

— Stephen Hawking

More than anything from this book I want you, the reader, to walk away feeling more empowered and with a greater sense of possibility. It isn't until we really connect to the realm of possibility can we even begin to move in the direction of what we can really do and achieve.

Believing is seeing and so is doing. You see, what is important to understand is that you aren't just a single person out there chugging along haphazardly helping people to become smarter and to feel better; rather, you are a part of a bigger conspiracy that involves a whole host of known and unknown factors at work for the greater good to come into manifestation.

Thinking you are all alone is like thinking you only have one cell that makes up the entirety of your body. The body is made up of a hundred trillion cells most of which are all working in harmony to keep the body functioning and healthy in spite of the things we do to it and put in it.

Life on this planet is organized in this same way. The majority of the energy of the planet is being directed towards the greater good, the health of the planet, and well-being. Though on the surface, we are the most obese, over-medicated, alcoholic, drug addicted, and mentally unwell collection of beings on the planet in history. This makes us the ripest we've ever been in our desire for our well-being. It isn't until you know war that you can truly desire peace. It isn't until you explore fear that you can really appreciate being soothed into relaxation. It is when you are drowning that you most want to breathe.

All over the planet there are people like you and me striving to help others and to make humanity healthier, smarter, and feel good more of the time. There are many who want to be helped and there are also many that don't want our help and are confused by the pain they suffer. What matters is that we work on ourselves and help those that are ready. When we do that, the system as a whole changes.

You are a part of a league of guides, teachers, and agents of change. They are all over the planet writing, speaking, teaching, training, and leading organizations. Each of us together is contributing to this process. Some have come into the awareness of their role and others are acting simply from an impulse and a calling. There is an invisible force working through all of us as if God dressed servants in rags and asked them to join those that suffer and help them to come home.

Each of us has been touched by these people. They too have been through the suffering and the pain that this physical world brings with it, just as we have. We all share in the suffering of this world no matter where, or to whom, you were born. This is the common bond of humanity. Money cannot protect you from it and neither can unconditional love. We are these servants when we fully embrace this work.

This world in all of its physicality is not real. It is a theatre, a stage, a stadium, a playground, a library, and a temple. It, and all things within it, are constantly changing through birth, life, and death. It is fleeting and inconsistent. It is an illusion. When you embrace the temporary reality of this physical plane, embrace your eternal nature, and connect with the divine you allow your true nature and purpose to come forth through you. The truth shall set you free.

This is a rare place for creativity, growth, and expansion. It is an incubator to support the soul —which is what we truly are— to develop and build upon the energy that we are. The most powerful and rewarding way to do that is to assist others in this process. This does not make you a master, but it certainly builds upon your soul's journey. There isn't a client you won't serve that won't touch and impact your life just as much as you touch theirs.

What I'm asking you to do is to become the best version of you, to commit to this unending journey and to connect to the eternal part of you. I'm also asking you to commit to the broader, non-physical part, the divine that is molding everything into place for all of us. Work from this perspective and to lead and guide through the inspiration and impulses that comes from this place.

Surrender your unworthiness, your need for perfection, and your shame for things done in the past so you can embrace your whole heart. Live in your authenticity and be real and vulnerable with the world. When you know with complete and total certainty that this is temporary and when you reach the other side of this life, you won't be judged and punished, rather celebrated for the experience you created, the lessons you learned, and the contribution you made.

God, the Universe, whatever you want to call it doesn't come out with a big red pen and start marking up your life like those ignorant teachers did. Sure there is contemplation about how you could have done things differently, but the focus will be placed more on how you woke up, the miracles you created, the fun you had, the life you lived, and the love you experienced and shared. Life is about these small ordinary moments of joy and the creativity and growth that you create and inspire others to have.

Make your life about the good stuff. Do the best you can and follow your heart's desire. It won't lead you the wrong way. This isn't to say that it will be easy, or that life will always be like walking through a beautiful flower garden, but it can be. You will make mistakes, screw it up, fall flat on your face, and bad things will happen, I promise you. What matters is that you are better because of it, and who you become in those moments, and as a result of them.

The most important part of all of this is that you learn and teach others to feel good more of the time. This is the true magic of life. Become a master at inducing and milking the joy out of life and when you do feel good take complete and total advantage of it. When you think you are there go even deeper into these good feelings so much so that you wonder to yourself how much better can it get and then, it does.

Yes I've made a good living in this business and as a result have created incredible freedom, enjoyed a variety of experiences, and have traveled the world. It is all wonderful and delicious. I love working one-on-one with my private clients. I do, it is fun, enjoyable, and we create awesome relationships.

When I step in front of a group of people I know that my reach is going even further. The cherry on top is that when I work with you, the coaches, the change agents, the league of extraordinary influencers, I get the thrill of knowing by helping you to create a better life, that you will go out and over your lifetime touch hundreds, thousands, millions, or even billions of more souls in the same way. The thrill comes from being a part of the bigger vision and thriving as a result.

No matter who you work with you are doing this too. This is what I'm asking you to do is to merge with your purpose and passion for the greater impact of this work.

Some time ago I was wondering what my next step should be in my development, both personally and professionally. I decided to do an inquiry and check in through meditation. The unique cover of a book, that I had read a decade before, flashed in my vision. I remembered immediately that the book was about a training process that involved being connected to neuro-feedback computers and would use the feedback to train you how to create deep states of alpha brainwaves.

When I read the book a decade earlier I was interested in the training though my mindset and belief system at the time wouldn't allow for me to invest in the kind of money, time, or the travel to Palo Alto, California where the training took place. When the book came into my awareness that day in meditation I answered yes to the impulse immediately. I couldn't remember the name of the book or the author, but I knew that I would find out and attend the earliest training I could make it to.

A few days went by and I was at my boyfriend's mom's house making dinner. When she got home she came in excited announcing that she had found an old friend that had moved to Sedona where we lived. She had met him years before because they both belonged to Marshal Thurber's Positive Deviants group. Curious, I asked about him. She said "Oh, you would love him. He's a scientist and a Doctor. He has this machine that he hooks you up to and uses the brainwaves to teach you how create different states, it's amazing!"

This was sounding very familiar. Strangely familiar, in fact, the timing was uncanny. I asked her what his name was and I googled it. It was Dr. James V. Hardt, the author of the book *The Art of Smart Thinking* which I had read a decade before and had just seen the cover of in my recent meditation. I contacted Dr. Hardt and found out he had moved his training center just a year before to a location five minutes from my home in Sedona. Three days later I was sitting in his seven day Alpha 1 training.

The process was powerful and life changing. It is unlike anything I could even begin to explain. When you work in the higher states of consciousness and do the healing work that comes along with it, to say you come out the other side of it changed, is an understatement. You come out of it a new person.

Even more powerful is that as I participated fully in the process, going through my own work and occasionally adding to the experience of the other participants, as I would in any relationship, Dr. Hardt recognized that I had something more to contribute to him and his company. He hired me to coach him personally and professionally and to redesign the training program he had been using for over twenty years. He also hired me to train staff in all three of his international locations to sell better and to be even more powerful in their change process with clients.

I'm not telling you this story to impress you, rather to demonstrate how far one can come, when working within the greater vision. When I embarked on this process I was a criminal, emotionally broken, and a disaster. A decade before I couldn't wrap my mind around putting myself into the Alpha 1 training and now I was leading its next expansion and the evolution to make it even more powerful, effective, and efficient.

What created this was part intention and part surrendering to the Universe and following the impulse of inspiration. There is within each of us a calling that comes from our heart's desire to bring us deeper into the many purposes we will fill over our lifetimes. When you feel this tugging at you, see that vision and hear that calling, your job is to answer to it. No matter how hard, how much you think it will cost, or how painful you think it might be, or how impossible it may seem, answer that call, take that first step and the path will be there to meet you. The Universe will provide the way, the resources, the teachers, and the solutions. All you've got to do to begin is to answer the big why, the strong motivation that is calling you, showing you, and molding it all into place. The mystery of "*How*" is the fun part that is guaranteed to come from your commitment.

You can refuse all of this, if you would prefer, because this is a Universe of freewill. Many souls have arrived at the end of their lives on Earth to find out they mucked it up and missed the point. They didn't answer to the hundreds and thousands of impulses to move in the direction of opening up to the most successful version of themselves. They know they could have done better, been smarter, loved more, been more creative, had more fun, grown more, and helped others than they did. What I'm asking you to do is to say *yes* to more of these things in life and appreciate them when they come in. Teach and guide others in your life to do this too. The world is becoming a better place and you are either a parasite sucking life out of it, or you are a part of the greater vision that is restoring it to well-being.

CONCLUSION

What inspired me to start this book in the first place was the need to get as much information to the people I wanted to influence to become successful coaches as quickly and efficiently as possible. When you spread this information over a six month relationship, through ninety minute, one-on-one sessions you don't have as much impact as you could in a book, workshop, or seminar. The mind learns best quickly.

For years I started and stopped a series of books. What got me to finish this book was getting over the need for it to be perfect. Perfection is a very unrealistic goal and only sets you up for disappointment. You'll never please everyone or get it exactly right. The day I surrendered all attachment to this book being any good at all was the day that I was able to sit down and write. As a result I wrote this book in four days, from the heart, and at such a rapid clip I didn't have time to think; just felt my way through it.

This book is a foundational starting point. You could easily study it at length, implement what you've learned, and thrive as a coach. I know because this is in essence the story of how I initially created success in this industry. I took the valuable components that I learned as a server in fine dining, a professional in finance, and an entrepreneur, what worked for me on my journey, and duplicated them into a coaching model. Over time I added in what I found was missing from my experience as a coach and my education with NLP®. There is much more to this story than what could even fit within this book's pages.

There are so many resources, technologies, processes, techniques, and strategies that couldn't be mentioned in this book because of the depth and breadth of the topics. For example hypnosis, trance, and NLP® are all very important to influencing others to change. Even this book includes a trance to guide you unconsciously to success as a coach, yet how it works isn't discussed in detail here. This is because these topics are best learned in a live seminar setting with us and in a group where you get to use what you learn with a variety of people from all walks of life.

Our system is not the only way. It may not even be the best way, but it is what I did to become successful, and it has been taught to many others who have become great and made a good living doing it. This system has proven over time that it creates measurable, duplicable success. As Richard Bandler says "You know a toaster works because it toasts the bread." Alliance Coaching works because it has created successful coaches and changed clients lives for the better time and time again.

What is important for you to understand is that you aren't in this alone and you don't have to do it alone either. Take what you learn in this book and implement it with what you already know works well. I highly recommend that you come to one of our courses, retreats, certification seminars, or consider joining our team to get you what you want out of life more quickly and intelligently.

I have waited until this point to make these suggestions because I wanted this book to be designed to help you build and grow your business and to help your clients. That is what is really important. I am of course biased about our coaching system, our trainings, and NLP® as the platform to influence others to change because again, it gets the job done, and done quickly, efficiently, and consistently. These are all important factors when charging others to help them to get the life they want.

Learning, growing, and improving ourselves is a never ending process. Personally I have attended hundreds of workshops, seminars, and retreats all over the world and will probably attend thousands more in my lifetime. The main reason I continue attending these kinds of trainings is because I find great pleasure in learning how the mind works and how successful people think. I'm also obsessed with the development of our species and how the planet is in transformation. Something inside me tells me that I came here to be a part of this special time in history for a very important reason.

There is also this part of me that craves so very much to walk alongside the very best as we usher in the change that is literally transforming this planet. In many ways I believe this transformation is what will save us from what otherwise would be our self-inflicted demise.

If you want to be among the best, be smarter, enjoy life more, and want to usher in this new era I strongly recommend that you contact us and learn more about what we can do together. The very best is yet to come, and I thank you for all that you are doing to influence that into becoming a reality.

Dustin Vice

POST SCRIPT FROM THE EDITOR

The changes I have made in my life as a result of Dustin's coaching have been so dramatic and wonderful, that I can still recall vividly, every word, of our first powerful conversation together. He understood me immediately and deeply, and showed me right away that he was ferocious about getting the best out of me, and tenacious about making even my wildest dreams come true.

At the time I was a Professor of English at Humboldt State University, and was lucky enough in that highly competitive world, to have landed a job in my own specialty, and at a University in an area where I wanted to live. In fact, I had just been awarded tenure, so it was a position that one would be very foolish to walk away from.

I felt a deeper calling though. I had recently turned my life around after a difficult divorce through working with a coach, and it was clear to me that I was being called to transition careers and move into coaching full time. The coach I was working with at the time had been in the field for many years, and was a fabulous coach, but had few clients and little income. That was, until she met Dustin and hired him.

"You have what it takes, Corey." She said enthusiastically, "And if you want to be a successful coach, the one thing you need to do, is work with Dustin. He tripled my income the first year I worked with him. He'll teach you what you need to know."

So, upon her recommendation I called Dustin and I told him:

"I have a three-year plan mapped out, for how I can transition away from the university, and replace my income in three years. That's what I want to do."

Then Dustin asked, with a certainty that was contagious, "How about if we cut that time in half and double the income? How does that sound?"

I hired him at that moment, and that is exactly what we did. Only a few months later I was announcing my resignation, and one year later I was no longer at the university, and was running a thriving private practice, changing lives one conversation at a time, and living the life of my dreams.

Everyone I told in the world of Academia thought I was crazy. Many were also envious and asked "How did you slip out of the golden noose?" It was clear that many wanted to do other things, but there was so much fear around making the change, taking the leap, and being unsuccessful.

Early on in our work, Dustin installed in me, using my own resources, an incredibly powerful degree of certainty, a depth of knowing and confidence that rose from my core, an unshakeable certainty of my success, so that I would have the courage, charisma and determination to succeed in my new endeavor. I still enjoy recalling a conversation with my Department Chair and the Dean of my College where this certainty surfaced. They both were so kind and concerned, that they asked: "Why don't you take a leave of absence for a year, and try the coaching thing out, and if it doesn't work out, we will have to hire you back. You won't risk losing your job permanently."

And while I truly appreciated their concern, I replied, with unshakeable certainty: "Thank you, that's very kind, but you know, when Hernando Cortez landed in the Americas, his men were about to mutiny. So, he ordered that all the ships be burned and sunk in the harbor: 'Burn the Ships! Now, there is no going home, except by going forward, to victory.' He cried. Well, I don't want any back doors, I don't need the option of retreat, it is only forward, onward to victory for me. That's why I have to quit and can't take a leave of absence."

There is nothing more powerful than certainty, nothing more valuable as a coach than the certainty of knowing you can be successful yourself, while you succeed at finding new clients and changing the lives of your existing clients.

And for any coach in the field today, I can tell you from direct experience, there is no faster, more effective, and enjoyable way to becoming the coach you were meant to be than riding the wave formed by the Alliance Coaching System.

I hope this book helps you in your practice, as you help others, and even more importantly, I hope you contact us at Alliance Coaching System so we can work together to enhance our impact on the world.

Here's to you and those you serve. Changing the world, one powerful conversation at a time!

Corey Lee Lewis

RECOMMENDED RESOURCES

Websites

AllianceCoachingSystem.com

MakingWavesTheBook.com

Books

Bandler, Richard, *Get the Life You Want* (Harper Collins Publishers 2008)

Bandler, Richard, *Trance-formations* (Health Communications 2008)

Hill, Napoleon, *Think and Grow Rich* (Wilder Publications 2007)

Newton, Michael, *Destiny of Souls* (Llewellyn Publications 2001)

Chapman, Gary, *Five Love Languages* (Northfield Publishing 2010)

Andrew, Douglas, *Missed Fortune* (Warner Books 2002)

Talbot, Michael *Holographic Universe* (Harper Collins Publishers 1991)

Moorjani, Anita, *Dying to be Me* (Hay House Publications 2012)

Katie, Byron, *Loving What Is* (Three Rivers Press 2002)

Villodo, Alberto, *Shaman, Healer, Sage* (Harmony Books 2000)

Coelho, Paulo, *The Alchemist* (Editoro Rocco Ltd 1988)

Zukov, Gary, *The Seat of the Soul* (Simon & Schuster 2014)

Deida, David, *The Way of the Superior Man* (Sounds True Inc. 2004)

ABOUT THE AUTHOR

Dustin Vice began his professional career in the world of finance. An underdog from the beginning with no college degree, or formal training, Dustin's success came about from his own unique ability to connect with people, and to discover the most successful strategies from the smartest people in his industry. In this high paced, high stakes world, Dustin learned three of the most useful things that he brings to Coaches today: first, how to make money through masterfully selling and influencing others to create powerful and lasting change; second, how to organize and manage a professional practice; and third, how to be a successful entrepreneur and work less hours a week than most have in their life.

While working in finance, Dustin found he was asked to coach and mentor others, both professionally and personally. His success as a Coach and mentor, and the deep fulfillment he got out of helping others to optimize themselves and their lives, led Dustin to begin coaching full time.

As his practice thrived, other Coaches, many of whom had been in the field for years, were drawn to Dustin, in dire need of his professional help. For example, the first Coach that hired Dustin to mentor her tripled her income within the first year of working with him. From this success other Coaches came and also Succeeded.

Recognizing both the number of coaching systems and institutions out there that have huge gaps in their curriculum, or even worse, their trainings aren't even worth the paper the certifications are printed on, and the current explosive growth in the coaching industry, Dustin founded the Alliance Coaching System (ACS) to teach both the fundamentals of coaching and business.

Today, he and his team of Ambassador Coaches from ACS are helping others to in the coaching industry to catapult their new and existing practices to supreme levels of success and to become wealthy. As a Licensed Master Practitioner and Licensed Trainer of Neuro-Linguistic Programming (NLP), Dustin continues to work as a trainer under Dr. Richard Bandler, the Co-creator of NLP, in events all over the world, and applies this highly effective technology to the business of coaching and selling.

Your Free Gifts

Included with this Book are Two **Powerful** Gifts to **Change** Your Life & Your Business

BONUS #1 Private One-on-One Strategy Session with Dustin Vice

CLAIM YOUR GIFT NOW

www.AllianceCoachingSystem.com/Session

BONUS #2 "Coaching Machine" Trance Meditation MP3 Download

Shift the Processes of Your Unconscious Mind Through this Hypnosis Recording to Dramatically Improve Your Skills, Confidence, and Success in Your Coaching Business

CLAIM YOUR GIFT NOW
www.MakingWavesTheBook.com/Downloads

Thank You!